BEYOND SUFFERING

BEYOND SUFFERING

Encountering Christ in the Book of Job

JOHN HARRIES

authorHOUSE®

AuthorHouse™ UK
1663 Liberty Drive
Bloomington, IN 47403 USA
www.authorhouse.co.uk
Phone: 0800.197.4150

NIV
Scripture quotations marked NIV are taken from the Holy Bible, New
International Version®. NIV®. Copyright © 1973, 1978, 1984 by
International Bible Society. Used by permission of Zondervan. All rights
reserved. [Biblica]

Published by AuthorHouse 11/13/2014

ISBN: 978-1-4969-9551-3 (sc)
ISBN: 978-1-4969-9552-0 (e)

Library of Congress Control Number: 2014919773

Dedication

For Judith, my wife and soul mate
and our three beautiful daughters Becky, Millie and Abi

Contents

Beyond Suffering: Encountering Christ in the Book of Job

Introduction

On 31st January 2000, Harold Shipman was pronounced guilty of killing fifteen patients under his care by lethal injection of diamorphine. It is believed that spanning 23 years as a GP in Hyde and Todmorden, Shipman murdered between 215-260 vulnerable elderly people. The day following his conviction I hosted a memorial service at St. George's Church, Hyde, for the victim's families. The church was packed as people came to pour out their grief and seek answers for the pain and hurt they were suffering. I confess I felt numb and to this day I struggle to find any words that can bring lasting comfort and spiritual healing to those families and friends. I mentioned in that service that 'our innocence had been destroyed,' and it had in so many ways; our faith in the medical profession, our confidence in our judgement of character for all maintained he was a caring, compassionate doctor, and for some the belief that God would keep them safe from harm. Maybe in time we might find reasons to explain why Harold Shipman had committed such ruthless acts of violation, but why had God allowed him to get away with these murders for so long and cause so many such pain and distress?

This question I have wrestled with for the last fourteen years both in my capacity as a parish priest and also in my personal life, as time and time again I have been forced to confront the enigma of innocent suffering and a loving omnipotent God. I empathise with Bertrand Russell, sharing his feeling of helplessness, when he wrote in the prologue to his autobiography[1],

> *'Echoes of cries of pain reverberate in my heart.*
> *Children in famine, victims tortured by oppressors,*
> *helpless old people a burden to their sons, and the*
> *whole world of loneliness, poverty, and pain make*
> *a mockery of what human life should be. I long to*
> *alleviate this evil, but I cannot, and I too suffer.'*

How is one to make sense of suffering? Why do bad things happen to good people? How can an almighty, all loving God allow the innocent and the vulnerable to suffer?

From the earliest times the dilemma posed by the suffering of innocent godly people has perplexed the world's greatest philosophers and theologians. Augustine advocated suffering was an inevitable consequence of free will, a view adopted by many today who argue our pains are the result of humanity's inhumanity. Whilst this argument may be plausible in some cases, there are difficulties in employing free will as an explanation for all suffering. For example, it fails to provide a satisfactory response to natural disasters - on average 250,000 people will die each year as a direct result of earthquakes, tornados and tsunamis, leaving millions more homeless and destitute. More disturbingly, free will, as generally understood, grants humanity a god-like status whereby every man, woman or child can seemingly frustrate and overrule the desires of an omnipotent creator. It is this aspect that troubled me most in the case of Dr. Shipman, for whilst he may think he had the power of God, I could not accept his belief as absolute. Far from free will providing a defence of faith, I found it actually undermines the belief that God is able to protect his people. A similar case can be made to answer those who advocate Satan as the architect of all suffering, envisioning a dualistic universe in which God is in constant conflict with his arch adversary. God is either Lord of all or he is not Lord at all, as Isaiah writes, under the inspiration of the Holy Spirit,

> *'this is what the Lord says...*
> *I am the Lord, and there is no other.*
> *I form the light and create darkness,*
> *I bring prosperity and create disaster;*
> *I, the Lord, do all these things.'* Isaiah 45:1, 7

However much we might want to exonerate God from any involvement in our suffering, we must not supplant his authority by appealing to free will or the machinations of some angelic being. We cannot see him as one who is constantly, desperately seeking to patch up his creation, helpless to stop the onslaught of evil and the wickedness of humanity. God is God and there is no other. He does as he pleases and all his ways are righteous and loving. The problem before us is how to reconcile this truth with the suffering of the innocent and the impression that those who flagrantly disobey God seem to flourish and thrive?

We need answers, but so often we are told that we will only understand when we get to heaven. That may be true, but still we need to try to make sense of our pain and suffering; we need to know whether or not God truly cares. For the Christian, it's not about his power to save, that's a given; it's about his love! The book of Job has been written specifically to address these questions, not theoretically, but through the lived out example of a blameless God fearing man. In Job the author explores the human dilemma, exposing the inadequacy of our moralistic worldview and replacing it with a biblical theology of God and suffering. Furthermore, he achieves this by making Job in his suffering, the focus of all our confusion, anger and pain, so that through Job we encounter our own personal struggles expressed in words as deep as our anguish, challenging God with a holy boldness we dare not match. Job becomes our spokesman, voicing our fears and our pain. It is by walking with him through his questioning that we discover not only answers to our deepest needs, but also hope and the strength to endure. For this reason I have not sought to provide numerous biographical stories of individual suffering, as it is not for us to interpret God's intentions in the lives of others, but instead to gain wisdom in our journey with Job, as the one, whose story God has specifically given us for our instruction and benefit.

As we consider the book of Job we need to bear in mind it was written pre-Christ, so the writer is trying to make sense of the world and God's dealings with man, but without seeing the full picture. This can be a help to us, for in times of trial we often need to strip everything back to the basics and start again from the beginning. It can help us to understand why it is we believe what we believe. I remember once driving through thick fog along the motorway, with no sat nav to guide me; only the rear lights of the car ahead and the cats-eyes marking the lanes and showing when I had finally reached the slip road. Sometimes, our suffering can be like driving through a thick fog. It concentrates our minds on what is most important; we ignore the scenery, we stop all careless conversation and we give all our attention to looking for signs of those who have gone before and for a sure guide to lead us home (Psalm 119:105). As we turn to Job, we will find that sure guide: We will walk with him through the fog of his understanding, but we also have the torch of the New Testament as our guide and the light of Christ at our side. It is my personal prayer that as we wrestle with the issues surrounding Job's suffering, we will come to experience, even as Job, the depth of God's love so that even in our most painful suffering, we might be able to worship him as the one who holds us in his everlasting arms.

Not much is known about the book other than what it tells us. It is unclear when it was written, although most scholars argue for it being postexilic or written during the exile in Babylon. The Jews have had difficulty placing it in the OT, not knowing whether it was historical or part of the wisdom tradition. It is also unclear whether Job and his friends were real or simply characters employed by the author to address the particular issue of righteous suffering. Personally, I don't think it is necessary to know whether or not Job actually existed. Indeed, in some ways treating him as a character can help to get past the tragedy in his life and its fairy-tale conclusion, allowing us to reflect more deeply on the posed theological issue. Throughout the book, Job is shown to have an in depth knowledge of Israelite theology and religious practice, but that does not mean he was necessarily Jewish. Indeed, many commentators suggest he was a resident of Edom and perhaps a descendent of Esau. Be that as it may, it seems clear that the author has chosen to describe Job and his dilemma within a Jewish believing framework to enable his readers to fully identify with the catastrophe that befalls Job. However, the relevance of this story is not limited to a Jewish audience. Job is simply presented as a moral god-fearing man, through whom we too can come to a deeper understanding of God's love for us in the midst of our own trials.

Historically the book is set in the East, which at that time was synonymous with the seat of wisdom (1 Kings 4:30). Job is declared in the opening verses to be 'the greatest man among all the people of the East,' intimating he was considered the epitome of wisdom and knowledge. The author is informing his readership that within the following narrative is distilled the wisdom of the finest minds of the ancient world. The general consensus is that Job aims to 'flesh out' what it means to live wisely, walking in the fear of the Lord. Moberly[2] has helpfully distinguished between living well in a general sense, as described in the book of Proverbs, and exemplifying wisdom in the midst of affliction, which is the central theme of Job. In particular he raises the view that such wisdom is not solely the possession of God, a view proposed by Davidson[3], but is also received through revelation by those who by faith apprehend God. I would go further arguing that in Job, wisdom is not presented in the abstract, but anticipates Christ, inasmuch as through the character of Job we discover Christ as the embodiment of wisdom and the one in whom believers are to find salvation in the midst of suffering. As Paul so eloquently writes in 1 Corinthians 1:30, *'it is because of him that you are in Christ Jesus, who has become for us wisdom from God – that is, our righteousness, holiness and redemption.'*

Tackling Job will not be easy intellectually or emotionally. It will be mind stretching and soul searching and, like the author of Job, I make no apology for that because suffering is not to be explained away with trite and trivial statements. Deep wounds are not healed with superficial plasters. They must first be searched and cleansed thoroughly by the word of God before lasting healing can begin. We must be prepared to allow God's word to search us and to transform our understanding that we might be able to test and approve God's will for our lives (Romans 12:2). We must be prepared to sit down with Job, to empathise with him, to plead our case alongside him and to wait upon the Lord with him.

In working through Job, I have endeavoured to treat the chapters as a progression of thought. My reason for doing so is to explore the many emotional, philosophical and ethical issues individuals have with the notion of suffering, before unpacking the Lord's response to Job in the final chapters. This may leave you frustrated at certain points, because in times of difficulty all we want is answers, but I would urge you to demonstrate Job's patience. This book is not a detailed theological treatise, of which there is a wealth of excellent commentaries on the market. Instead, this constitutes a series of meditations based on sermons given to my church congregation, with the passionate desire to encourage them in their trials and direct them to a closer walk with Jesus. My sincere hope is that in reading this exploration of Job you will not only find some of the answers you seek to the question of suffering, but more importantly, you will be brought to a place where God can speak directly into your personal situation and assure you of his love and power to save. Finally I pray that you will arrive at the point where, despite everything, you can experience God's peace in your life and be enabled to entrust yourself wholeheartedly to the one who has loved you passionately from all eternity and to his Son who freely, lovingly gave his life for you.

My sincere thanks are due to a number of individuals who read early drafts of this manuscript and provided invaluable advice.

In particular I am indebted to Trevor Hodson and Michael Walters, who advised and encouraged me through the early stages, as well as to my wife Judith, without whose continued support this book would never have seen the light of day. I am also grateful to my congregation at St. John's, Walton for their enthusiastic response to the sermon series on Job that formed the backbone of this work. Finally, I would like to offer my heartfelt prayers to the people of Hyde and Todmorden, whose suffering prompted my search for answers. I cannot presume to say I have found what you seek, but I do hope and pray that in walking with Job, you may find some measure of comfort and peace.

1. Bertrand Russell (1975) Prologue: What I have lived for. George Allen & Unwin Ltd, London
2. Moberley, RWL (2013) Old Testament Theology: Reading the Hebrew Bible as Christian Scripture. Baker Academic Grand Rapids Michigan, 266
3. Davidson, AB (1895) The Book of Job. Cambridge University Press, 200-210

CHAPTER 1

God's man in the East (Job 1:1-5)

One of the more painful aspects of witnessing innocent suffering is the sense of God's betrayal. Everyday we turn on our TV's or open our newspapers to discover innocent bystanders have been murdered or kidnapped; children have been sold into slavery, exploited by human traffickers; honest hardworking lives have been destroyed by natural disasters, hurricanes, earthquakes and tsunamis; thousands of victims of civil war are dying from malnutrition and disease; and benevolent believers are being persecuted and tortured for their faith. It strikes many as the height of injustice, when they also see the violent, the immoral and the wicked flourish, to all appearances without a care in the world. The sense of betrayal becomes anger at God for seeming to stand by and do nothing. Heartbroken by the plight of our fellow human beings, we take matters into our own hands, setting up relief programmes and such like, but always there is the assault on our faith amid a growing frustration – if God is all powerful and all loving why doesn't he do something! Many feel betrayed by the Church because from their earliest years it has pedalled the doctrine that God loves and cares for us – but from their perspective there is no ground for justification - God is distant, God is disinterested, God is a disappointment.

Consequently, when we turn to the opening chapter of the story of Job and read of a man who is blameless and upright, god-fearing and devout, wealthy and successful, we instinctively know what is going to happen. Like all fairy tales we know that the idyllic scene will not last, but will be supplanted by harsh reality: Evil will arise and God will not be there to help! If Sunday school has taught us anything it is that the tales of David and Goliath, Noah and the Flood, Jesus healing the Blind man, the feeding of the 5,000 and countless other miracles are the stuff of legend. They are stories that may have happened to other people, but they do not happen today, not to us anyway. So where does that leave us in terms of our relationship with a caring, compassionate all conquering Creator?

God's point of view

One of the biggest difficulties we face in trying to make sense of the suffering of the righteous is that, like Job, we tend to put ourselves at the centre of all that is happening and therefore see everything from our perspective rather than God's. Our frustration and disappointment with God cause us to become so judgemental that often we find it hard to hear what God is saying. Jesus puts it this way in speaking of those who criticise others, *'why do you look at the speck of sawdust in your brother's eye and pay no attention to the plank in your own eye? You hypocrite, first take the plank out of your own eye, and then you will see clearly'* (Matthew 7:3,5). If this is true of the way we relate to each other, then how much more it applies in our questioning of God. To understand why a loving God should permit good people to suffer we need to be prepared to lay aside our prejudices, resentment and hurt so that we may listen carefully to all God has to say in his defence.

The first step in this process is to start at the very beginning with an understanding of who we are before our Creator: For Job and for us it means returning to our origins. In the opening verses we are told that Job is the *'greatest man among the people of the East'* (1:3). This seemingly innocuous statement is full of importance for it takes us to the heart of mankind's predicament and God's graciousness.

Why is the 'East' important?

The East, as a theological concept, holds great significance in that it represents those who are outside of God's covenantal presence and therefore separated from God's chosen people. Geographically, it represented the land beyond the Jordan rift valley, the western boundary of Israel, encompassing the lands of Midian, Edom, Moab, Babylon and Assyria further towards the north. It was to the east that Abraham sent the sons of his concubines so they would not be included in the inheritance of Isaac (Genesis 25:6). During the time of the kings, the land of Uz was often associated with the land of Edom (Lamentations 4:21), a place outside of God's holy land, and occupied by Esau's descendants, disinherited through

Esau despising his birth right (Genesis 25:29-34). It was to Babylon, the symbol of all that is opposed to God (Revelation 17:1-6), that Israel was exiled because of their sin against the Lord. Adam and Eve, banished from God's presence, were sent by God to the East (Genesis 2:24) and following Cain's murder of Abel we are told, *'Cain went out from the Lord's presence and lived in the land of Nod, east of Eden'* (Genesis 4:16).

The East, therefore, theologically signifies a state of being in alienation from God and removed from his presence. From the outset, the author is informing his Israelite readership that Job is living amongst a people who are outside of God's covenant. Job's situation is not unlike that of Lot who chose to dwell among the people of Sodom, a righteous man in the midst of the ungodly (Genesis 13:10-13).

A clue in Job's name

This sense of alienation is further highlighted by Job's own name, which some commentators have translated, 'hated', proposing he was at enmity with God in his suffering with a more literal translation 'alienated,' or 'discovenanted[1].' Andersen suggests Job's name may originally have meant 'where is my father?' which is particularly significant in explaining Job's sense of abandonment by God. Names were of great importance in Israelite thought, and Job's name is highly symbolic as one who acutely feels his separation from God, the root problem in all his suffering, and an indication that Job may have been a Gentile believer. In his letter to the Ephesian church, the apostle Paul describes this state of alienation in terms of being bereft of hope, with no expectation of God's blessing,

> *'remember that at that time you were excluded from citizenship in Israel and foreigners to the covenants of the promise, without hope and without God in the world'*   Ephesians 2:12

If Job is being portrayed as living outside of the Promised Land among an ungodly people and consequently excluded from the promises of God, how is it possible he is blessed greatly by God (1:3) and hedged in by his love? How can he be held up as God's servant before Satan and all the hosts of heaven? Why does God single him out as one to be emulated?

God reaches into darkness

Firstly, Job is not the first person that God, in his wisdom and mercy, has called from the East, a state of spiritual estrangement, to be a servant of his will. God called Abram from Ur of the Chaldeans in the East to be the father of his people Israel (Genesis 11:27-12:5); Ruth was a Moabitess, yet she bore a son to Boaz, Obed the grandfather of David (Ruth 4:16-22), from whose line our Lord descended. God raised up Cyrus, king of the Medes and Persians, for the deliverance of his people from exile (Ezra 1:1-4) and by a star the Magi were summoned from the East that they might come and worship the Lord at his birth (Matthew 2:1,2). God does not overlook individuals or nations simply because they are spiritually in darkness. Quite the opposite! It is the mercy of God that he reaches out to those lost in darkness; he lifts up those who are cast down and breaks the chains of those who are imprisoned. God raised up Job to be his servant and to be a beacon to the nations and to us. Indeed, Calvin suggests his faith was a means of shaming the Israelites that they might more wholeheartedly turn back to their God and walk in his laws.[2] As Paul remarks,

> *'In as much as I am the apostle to the Gentiles, I make much of my ministry in the hope that I may somehow arouse my own people to envy and save some of them,'* Romans 11:13,14

Job seeks out God

Secondly, Job is blessed even though he is outside of God's covenant land, because God is love. He is gracious and compassionate, reaching out in mercy to each and every person whom he has created. As God had mercy on the Ninevites though Jonah sought their destruction (Jonah 4:1-3); as he showed compassion to the widow of Zarephath, raising her son to life through the prayer of Elijah (1 Kings 17:17-24); as he was gracious to Naaman, healing him of his leprosy (2 Kings 5:8-15); as he forgave the sin of his people Israel time and time again in the desert, so God calls sinners to repentance that he might bestow upon them the blessing of eternal life (2 Peter 3:9). If God reaches out to all, even the most rebellious, that they might be blessed with life, how much more should we expect the Lord to bestow his love upon one, such as Job, who seeks after him, even if lives among a people who are excluded from God's presence.

Far from being distant and disinterested in humanity, God is seen, from this perspective, to be fully committed to reaching out to those whom he has created, even though they are estranged through sin. It is unlikely Job fully appreciates this for, as we shall see later, he has come to expect God's blessing as his right for trying to live a blameless life. The worldview of Job and his friends is that whoever does good receives favour, whilst those who do evil will be punished. Such a view makes no concession to their state of alienation, by which they are all held in judgement. As the people in the time of Noah went about their own business completely ignorant of God until the floods came, so Job and his friends have little realisation that they are living 'outside of Eden.'

All humanity is alienated from God

As we reflect on the significance of Job's situation as God's man living in the East, it is helpful to consider how this applies to ourselves as Christians living in the world. The book of Genesis speaks of the fall of Man and the resulting expulsion of Adam and Eve from the Garden of Eden. As a consequence, scripture asserts that all mankind has grown up in alienation from God and is under condemnation (Romans 5:12-14). We are all, apart from Christ, theologically, children of the East! Furthermore, the bible tells us that we have all broken God's laws at one time or other so that we cannot put all the blame on our ancestors.

> 'As it is written, 'there is no-one righteous, not even one; there is no one who understands, no one who seeks after God. All have turned away, they have together become worthless; there is no one who does good, not even one"   Romans 3:10-12

Living outside of Eden, strangers to God's covenant promises and walking in disobedience to his laws should mean we receive nothing from God, neither blessing nor protection. Like a child excluded from school or a family member denied an inheritance from a guardian's will, we cannot legitimately expect to receive any benefit from our disgrace. Moreover, far from being blessed, our only expectation should be that of judgement – suffering should be the norm rather than the exception. However, God in his mercy cannot bear to witness the suffering of those whom he has created in love, whatever their situation. For this reason he does not treat us as we deserve, but richly showers us moment by moment with his love, not withholding anything that might be for our benefit, even if we receive such gifts without acknowledgement or gratefulness! We may be separated from him, but we are ever in his thoughts. Each day, the Lord provides and cares for us in so many ways, as Jesus says of his Father, *'he causes his sun to rise on the evil and the good, and sends rain on the righteous and the unrighteous'* (Matthew 5:45). No matter who we are or what we think of him, God gives us the strength for each day, food to nourish us, friends to support us, challenges to help us grow, blessings to make us joyful and families to care for us – even those who are most ignorant of him and abuse him to his face: Our loving heavenly Father cannot stand idly by and watch even his most rebellious children suffer unduly.

Everything we have is a gift of grace

So often, like Job, we take God's blessings for granted and expect them as a right. If God were to remove his protection from us and cause us inconvenience, pain or grief we would and do become angry, just as a child might react to her parents if a favourite item was withheld for whatever reason. But the truth is, all we possess and enjoy has been given to us by God's grace and not on the basis of our merit. There are so many people in the world today who do not have enough food, who suffer with ill health or who have no family. Are we any better than they? No. Are we more deserving than they? No. Do we respect and honour God more than they do? No. Everything we have received is a gift of grace from a God who is under no obligation to provide for us, and whom many despise or deny his existence.

We see this truth most gloriously demonstrated in the person of our Lord Jesus Christ. For our Lord left the glory of the courts of heaven, and taking upon himself the form of a man, was born in a manger. He humbled himself, submitting to our frailty and to his Father's will. He surrendered himself to our abuse and malice, taking upon himself our sin and condemnation on the cross. He did this so that the barrier of hostility between God and ourselves could be removed forever and that we might be restored to Eden. He did this even though we were ignorant of our predicament and wilfully disobedient, as the apostle Paul declares, *'God demonstrates his own love for us in this: While we were still sinners, Christ died for us,'* (Romans 5:8).

God's love is not exclusive

I find this verse both a salutary reminder of my own arrogance and God's amazing love. Like the Pharisees who brought the woman caught in adultery to Jesus, there can be a tendency for those who are 'blessed' with a good life to pass judgement on others, as if they are somehow the authors of their own misfortune. But Jesus shows us that God's love is not exclusive; it is not reserved for the righteous and the clean living, for God sent his Son to save the outcast, the poor, the sick, the destitute, the widow and the orphan. When we pass by the beggar on the street, hardly noticing him, have we considered that God knows him by name and that Jesus died that he also might be saved? When we are filled with hatred over someone who has hurt us, do we realise that even as God grieves for our pain, he reaches out in love and forgiveness to our tormentor. There are occasions when I need to remind myself of this, when I speak out of turn, when I cause another hurt by my actions or when I dishonour the name of the Lord by my thoughts, words or deeds. At such times, as I ask for forgiveness, I take comfort that Jesus did not give his life just for the so called 'clean living,' but that he died that all might receive the gift of eternal life (John 3:16).

Furthermore, such love gives me hope that those I care for, who refuse to accept the Lord, can still be saved, for God does not give up on people easily. I remember my father being so bitter towards God for most of his life, so annoyed at me becoming a Christian, yet allowing me to pray for him on his death bed. Though he didn't say anything, I believe I saw a flicker of hope in his eyes, a glistening that said to me, 'I have made peace with God.' We should never give up praying for those around us, for God never gives up on them. But then, such is the magnanimity of God that he reaches out in love and compassion even to those whom we might struggle even to acknowledge; the reprobate, the violent and the criminal.

Nicky Cruz was just such a person, a Puerto Rican growing up on the streets of Brooklyn, he led the infamous Mau Mau gang, terrorising the neighbourhood. He hated everyone and everyone hated him. He hated God, blaming him for the life he had. Yet, God did not abandon him, but slowly by his grace he called Nicky to himself, through the preaching of David Wilkerson. Nicky's life was turned around. He writes in his autobiography 'Run, Baby, Run,' of his conversion,

'I went to my closet and took off my Mau Mau jacket and shoes and put them in a bag. 'No more,' I thought to myself. 'No longer will I need these.' I reached up to the shelf and took down my revolver. By force of habit I started to put the shells in the magazine so I could sleep with the gun on my night stand. But suddenly I remembered. Jesus loves me. He will protect me. I took the bullets and placed them back in the small box and put the gun back on the shelf. In the morning I would turn it in to the police. I walked by the mirror. I couldn't believe what I saw. There was a light coming from my face I had never seen before... I was happy. The burden of fear was gone. I could laugh. I knelt beside the bed and threw my head back. 'Jesus...' Nothing else came out. 'Jesus...' And finally the words came. 'Thank you, Jesus ... thank you.' That night, for the first time in my memory, I put my head on the pillow and slept nine beautiful hours. No tossing on the bed. No fear of sounds outside my room. The nightmares were gone[3]

Since that day the Lord has powerfully used Nicky's testimony in the lives of countless individuals, as proof that there is no pit so deep that God will not reach down in love to raise us up. The apostle Paul perfectly expresses this truth in proclaiming God's saving mercy to himself, as a clarion call to all who feel they are unworthy of God's grace,

> *'Here is a trustworthy saying that deserves full*
> *acceptance: Christ Jesus came into the world to save*
> *sinners – of whom I am chief. But for this very reason*
> *I was shown mercy so that in me, the worst of sinners,*
> *Christ Jesus might display his unlimited patience as*
> *an example for those who would believe on him and*
> *receive eternal life'* 1 Timothy 1:15,16

God loves you

The apostle John declares, *'this is love: not that we loved God, but that he loved us and sent his Son as an atoning sacrifice for our sins,'* (1 John 4:10). In other words, God so loves you that there is nothing you ever can do that would cause God to love you more; and there is nothing you can ever do that would cause God to love you less. God sent his one and only Son to die for you on a cross: What greater act of love could God ever bestow upon you! He could not love you any more even if you were to live a model life, walking in perfect obedience to his commands. Again, God sent his one and only Son to die for you when you did not love him and walked in disobedience to his laws. Since this is true, what could you do now to make him love you less? – nothing! God is love, as the sun is light. Just as the sun burns brightly sending its golden beams onto the earth each and every day, so God's love shines forth into our lives each and every moment, undiluted, unchanging, unconstrained. God's love is full on, it has no dimmer switch; it does not ebb and flow; it is not dependent upon us or on anything we do; it is purely and completely dependent on God and his grace. That is why God cannot stop loving us even when we are estranged from him and walking in darkness. The sun does not stop shining at night; we are just facing the other way. Likewise, when we walk in spiritual darkness it is not through God withdrawing his love, but because we are looking away from him. When we suffer it is not a sign that God has stopped loving us – that is impossible. Indeed, if God should allow us to suffer it is because he loves us so much.

Whoever we are, whatever we have done, we can be assured that God longs to take us into his loving arms. He is not dismayed by the blackness of our hearts nor is he confounded by the bleakness of our situation. Though estranged from him through sin, though undeserving of any good thing, still our heavenly Father calls to us and showers us with his love. We live outside of Eden, in a broken world, where there are natural disasters and human tragedies; where there is violence, hatred and immorality; where there is pain, suffering and grief, but through it all we are not alone. God has not abandoned us - he is not abandoning you. He loves you and he longs to be gracious to you. He has sent his one and only Son into the world for you - and his light and his love are sufficient for all!

1. Andersen, F.I. (1976) Job. Tyndale OT Commentaries. IVP Leicester, England, pg.78
2. Calvin, J. (1979) Sermons from Job. Baker Book House, Grand Rapids, Michigan, pg. 7
3. Nicky Cruz (1971) Run Baby Run: Hodder and Stoughton, London pg. 123

CHAPTER 2

Righteous Suffering (Job 1:6-2:10)

Our reason for studying the book of Job is that we might be able to make sense of the suffering of the righteous. We have no difficulty accounting for the misery of wrongdoers, for clearly they are receiving their just desserts, but innocent suffering seems inexplicable. In our lectionary the joy and hope of Christmas Day are instantly turned to despair and confusion on Holy Innocents day, when we recall the slaughter of unsuspecting boys less than two years of age by a vengeful Herod. How is this to be explained?

The essential premise on which the book of Job opens is that the righteous are protected and blessed by God and consequently should not suffer. This continues to be the world's assumed philosophy, whether or not people believe in God. One attempt to resolve this dilemma is to invoke a third party, a Satan, whose nature is undiluted evil and whose desire is to destroy all that God has created and make himself lord of all. In this form of dualism, the world becomes the battleground where these two rivals fight for supremacy, with humanity becoming the inevitable casualty of war. Such a view evokes thoughts of pagan mythology and presents humankind as a reluctant third party whose actions may tip the balance one way or the other. There is no biblical justification for this explanation of suffering, but it is noteworthy that just such a satanic figure is presented to us in the opening chapter of Job. In fact, satan is first introduced in Genesis 3:1, in the guise of a serpent, and alluded to in the prophesies of Isaiah 14:12-22 and Ezekiel 28:12-19, but his name is only explicitly mentioned in Job, where 'ha-sātān' better designates a role of accuser or opponent, rather than a specific character[1]. It is only in the New Testament, most notably by Jesus in Matthew 12:26 and Luke 22:31-32, that this accuser is personified, though numerous references abound throughout the gospels, Acts and the letters. However, whilst exercising great power, his might is inconsequential to that of Almighty God, and there is never any suggestion that Satan's schemes in any way hinder God's purposes. In the discussion that follows I have chosen to refer to 'ha-sātān' as Satan, in line with Jesus' later designation, simply because we are more familiar with this association, but as will be seen there is no suggestion of pagan dualism or power sharing in Satan's confrontation with God. Satan may be presented as the agent of Job's suffering but he is not the architect and his influence is strictly controlled.

Job – A model human being

Job is presented to us as the model human being, declared to be blameless and upright, fearing God and shunning evil. This is not simply the opinion of the author. God himself, before the entire angelic host, twice describes Job in identical fashion in his dispute with Satan;

> *'The Lord said to Satan, 'Have you considered my servant Job? There is no-one on earth like him; he is blameless and upright, a man who fears God and shuns evil'*   Job 1:8, 2:3

Job is another Abram, a godly man amongst men, through whom God has chosen to reveal himself. He is God's servant and of all the people in the East there is no one else like him. He is mentioned alongside Noah and Daniel in Ezekiel 14:14 as a man of renown and godly piety. He is a shining beacon of how humanity is to live under God and he is a stumbling block to Satan. In the Garden of Eden the serpent sought to destroy the work of God through the fall of man. Yet here is Job, re-establishing what Satan has tried so vehemently to destroy. Psalm 1 could very well have been written with Job in mind,

> *'Blessed is the man who does not walk in the counsel of the wicked or stand in the way of sinners or sit in the seat of mockers. But his delight is in the law of the Lord, and on his law he meditates day and night. He is like a tree planted by streams of water, which yields its fruit in season and whose leaf does not wither. Whatever he does prospers'*   Psalm 1:1-3

Job was blessed in his family, having seven sons and three daughters, the numbers seven and three representing completeness and perfection. In terms of his wealth he was equally prosperous, owning seven thousand sheep, three thousand camels, five hundred yoke of oxen and five hundred donkeys, as well as having a large number of servants. As such his life bore glorious testimony to the benefits of obedience to God – and Job knew it. Whenever his sons would hold a feast, Job would ensure that they were ritually purified afterwards, sacrificing a burnt offering for each of them and pledging their full commitment and devotion to God. He did this in case they had inadvertently sinned and cursed God whilst they were not fully in control of their thoughts and actions. Job wanted nothing to hinder the safety and prosperity of his family. He walked in the fear of the Lord, espousing wholeheartedly the words of the psalmist,

> *'How can a young man keep his way pure?*
> *By living according to your word.*
> *I seek you with all my heart;*
> *do not let me stray from your commands.*
> *I have hidden your word in my heart*
> *   that I may not sin against you.*
> *Praise be to you, O Lord, teach me your decrees.*
> *With my lips I recount all the laws*
> *   that come from your mouth.*
> *I rejoice in following your statutes*
> *   as one rejoices in great riches.*
> *I meditate on your precepts and consider your ways.*
> *I delight in your decrees;*
> *I will not neglect your word'*   Psalm 119:9-16

For this reason Job was honoured among the people as a man of God. His wisdom was respected, he was totally trustworthy and his prayers were answered before the throne of God. It was no surprise God should bless Job and make him *'the greatest man among the people of the East.'* In so doing, God was demonstrating what happens to those who trust him and walk in his ways. Job was a living testimony of God's faithfulness to his promises. Consequently, if anyone should be spared from suffering it is righteous, God fearing Job. As a father delights in his ideal son or an employer cherishes his model employee, so God must deal justly with those who are godly. He must protect his own, especially when they are his delight!

A relationship based on fear?

It is this association Satan would challenge, setting the scene for Job's misery:

> *'Does Job fear God for nothing? Have you not put a hedge around him and his household and everything he has? You have blessed the work of his hands, so that his flocks are spread throughout the land. But stretch out your hand and strike everything he has, and he will surely curse you to your face'* Job 1:9-11

Satan's argument is a serious attack on the nature of faith. Do people obey God because they are fearful of what may happen if they don't? Prior to the reformation Western medieval congregations were held in terror at the thought of being consigned to hell for their misdemeanours. Even today, many sincere people obey the commandments for fear of punishment rather than out of a genuine love for God. They fully appreciate the many blessings they have in life and dread that one-day these may be taken from them. For them the story of the man healed at the pool of Bethesda is a stark warning, *'Stop sinning or something worse may happen to you'* (John 5:14).

This is the power of Satan's argument. Everyone knows that God looks after Job. Although he lives outside of God's Promised Land, God has put a hedge round him and his family and he cannot be touched. But, Satan argues, Job's faith is self-serving – he does not love God but the blessings God provides. If God should turn a blind eye, allowing Job to suffer then his true colours will be revealed. Job doesn't love God; he's scared of God. Take away all his possessions, all his family and he will hate God forever.

I recall talking with a parishioner following the death of her son. She spoke of her faith when she was younger and happily married. Then her husband died after a particularly painful and distressing illness in which she cared for him at home, while raising their invalid son. As her son grew he became more independent and began to care for himself. At 28 years of age, for the first time in his life, he was permitted to go abroad with some friends for a couple days. On the final day the plane was delayed due to strike action, and while waiting her son went for a walk along the beach. Standing on a rock and looking out to sea, it appears he fell in and was taken by the tide. 'Why? Where was God?' she asked desperately. 'Why didn't God intervene? I thought he was my friend. I thought he would protect my family. How can I trust in a God who is so capricious? Is there a God at all?'

Does faith blind us to reality?

One of the principle reasons high profile atheists are so vitriolic in their attack on Christianity, is precisely because they see God as a betrayer of hope and a destroyer of dreams. They argue that religion is a prop and faith purely a desire that God you will give you what you cannot take for yourself. With much sincerity and bitterness they will swear 'faith is an illusion; it has no substance, because time and time again God has failed his people – and he will continue to fail you as he has failed me. Your faith has blinded you to reality.'

This is precisely the response that Satan desires. He doesn't simply want to destroy Job and make God look 'foolish' before all the courts of heaven. If he can bring Job to deny God's goodness he will be able to prove that faith in God is futile and empty of meaning. The stakes are high and God is not unaware of the responsibility he is placing upon Job's shoulders. In response to Satan's demand he hands his servant over (Job 1:12).

Within one day, all Job's children are killed and all his wealth is taken from him, either by marauders or natural disasters. It is impossible to underestimate the shocking impact this must have had on Job. His entire world has collapsed around him, without any warning whatsoever. We could easily understand if he packed up his bags and walked out on God.

Faith is more than fortune

Satan knows how to break people, but he has seriously misjudged Job. Contrary to Satan's prediction, Job does not curse God but responds,

> *'Naked I came from my mother's womb, and naked*
> *I shall depart. The Lord gave and the Lord has taken*
> *away; may the name of the Lord be praised'* Job 1:21

For Job, faith is more than fortune. Job desires God more than all his earthly possessions and happiness. His prayer is that of Asaph, the psalmist,

> *'Whom have I in heaven but you?*
> *And earth has nothing I desire besides you.*
> *My flesh and my heart may fail,*
> *But God is the strength of my heart and my portion*
> *for ever'* Psalm 73:26

and his song is that of Habakkuk,

> *'Though the fig tree does not bud*
> *and there are no grapes on the vines,*
> *though the olive crop fails*
> *and the fields produce no food,*
> *though there are no sheep in the pen*
> *and no cattle in the stalls,*
> *yet I will rejoice in the Lord, I will be joyful in God*
> *my Saviour'* Habakkuk 3:17, 18

Job refuses to turn away from God, despite the disaster that has befallen him and his family. He is completely in the dark concerning what has taken place in the heavenly realms, yet his faith remains firm. Job has not succumbed to Satan's malice and God is vindicated in his assertion.

The suffering deepens

Once again, we are taken to the courts of heaven, where Satan comes to present himself before the Lord. Once again God points out the righteousness of his servant Job, to which Satan responds, *'Skin for skin! A man will give all he has for his own life. But strike his flesh and bones and he will surely curse you to your face'* (Job 2:4). As if Job has not already suffered enough, God permits him to be afflicted with painful sores from head to toe. We find him scrapping himself with broken pottery as he sits in an ash heap; a picture of utter misery and despondency. Job's life, far from being an image of Eden, is more a picture of hell. God has withdrawn all his beneficial influence and Job is completely in the hands of Satan. I argued in the last chapter that we are all born under condemnation, outside of Eden. However, through God's mercy and grace we are shielded from the full horror of our separation. Without being alarmist, we now see through Job's affliction, what would happen should God remove all his protection and allow Satan free reign. Satan's malice is unquenchable! Job's wife urges him 'curse God and die.' Yet, once again, Job refuses to sin responding, *'Shall we accept good from God and not trouble,'* (Job 2:10).

On hearing of his troubles, Job's friends *'set out … to go and sympathise with him and comfort him,'* (Job 2:11). Yet, as they approached they barely recognised their friend, *'they began to weep aloud, and they tore their robes and sprinkled dust on their*

*heads. They sat with him for seven days and nights, not saying a
word, because they saw how great his suffering was'* (Job 2:12-13).

God is in control

We need to let the full horror of Job's situation touch our hearts.
Why has God allowed this? Has he been outmanoeuvred by
Satan and tricked into allowing Job to be humiliated before the
whole world? Does God simply desire to show off his prodigy,
as a way of taunting Satan? Is God callous in his treatment of
his servants? Such views are not supported by the author of
Job, neither are they consistent with the biblical revelation of
God's character. In seeking to understand Job's affliction, it is
essential we appreciate that in everything, God is in control
and his purpose is love for Job. It is God who introduces Job
to Satan in their conversation, not the other way around. God
is not somehow tricked by Satan or backed into a corner.
Although Satan believes himself to be the prime mover, he
is mistaken just as he was when Christ was condemned to
die on the cross. God's purposes are far beyond even Satan's
comprehension. God is not about to surrender his servant to
Satan's malice without some higher purpose or some greater
blessing. The God who says to his people,

> *'can a mother forget the baby at her breast
> and have no compassion on the child she has borne?
> Though she may forget, I will not forget you!
> See, I have engraved you on the palms of my hands'*
> Isaiah 49:15,16a

will not turn a blind eye to his loved one's pain or willingly
afflict the apple of his eye. To do such a thing would be to

join with Satan, partaking of his malice and destroying that which he has created in love. God is pure, holy, unconstrained, uncompromising love. He is not malicious, nor capricious; he is gracious and he grieves with us in our affliction. Over and over in the gospels we see Jesus deeply moved in the face of suffering. He shows compassion to those who are hungry (Matthew 15:32), he weeps over Jerusalem because the people did not know what would bring them peace (Luke 20:41,41), his heart goes out to a widow at the loss of her son (Luke 7:13), and at the grave of Lazarus he weeps (John 11:35).

Job is left in the dark

Job is not suffering because of some sin he has committed; no charge has been brought against him, even from his accuser. Job is suffering even though he is innocent. Some may argue on the basis of the heavenly dispute that the reason behind Job's suffering is to prove his faith genuine. This is surely part of the answer for scripture speaks of the quality of our faith being tested and refined through fire (1 Peter 1:7; 1 Corinthians 3:10-15). We can all think of godly men and women, who have come through periods of great struggle with a stronger, purer faith. Facing trials and temptations, often causes us to review our lives, refocus our priorities and recommit ourselves to the Lord: When all other supports are taken away, we are free to cling more tightly to Jesus. That said, there are still a lot of issues to be unpacked and worked through, a point clearly understood by the author, for it would appear that by Job 2:10, the argument between Satan and God has been settled. God has been vindicated and there is no more mention of Satan throughout the rest of the book. He has skulked away with his tail between his legs, humiliated by the integrity of Job's faith and the purity of his love for the Lord. We are left with Job's struggle to understand why he has suffered and what this means in terms of his relationship with the Lord. The birth of our first child was quite traumatic and although, in our case, everything turned out well, afterwards my wife had a lot of questions and issues that she needed to process. This is not unusual. In most cases, it is not the suffering itself, but the working through what it means in terms of our lives and our relationship with God that takes the time.

Job has been left completely in the dark regarding the reasons behind his suffering. If he had been made aware of all that had been discussed in the courts of heaven, he might well have felt some small sense of victory. Job has justified God's assessment of him and disproved Satan's assertion that his faith is self-serving and not authentic. But he is never made aware of the importance of his standing firm nor his fulfilment of God's trust, which we are to assume, is left for the glory of heaven. As it was for Job, surely it is true for you also if you are suffering for the gospel at this time. You do not know what discussions have taken place in the courts of heaven. You do not know what importance hangs on your standing firm in your faith. You do not know how many people will be strengthened in their faith and their walk with the Lord because of your testimony. You do not realise how much responsibility God has placed upon your shoulders. You do not know the praise in heaven that redounds to God because of your obedience – you only know that it hurts. Often, it's this lack of understanding that is the bitterest pill to swallow. If only we knew what our perseverance is achieving we could endure more courageously, but instead we are called to live by faith, to put our trust in God, look to the victory we have through Christ's resurrection (1 Corinthians 15:58) and fix our eyes on Jesus

'who for the joy set before him endured the cross,
scorning it's shame, and sat down at the right hand
of the throne of God. Consider him who endured
such opposition from sinful men, so that you will not
grow weary and lose heart.'   Hebrews 12:2,3

It is for this reason we need to journey with Job, engaging fully with his struggle, searching with him for answers and wrestling with him for God's blessing (Genesis 32:24-28). In walking with Job I pray you will discover the truths God would speak to you. Satan doesn't have some sort of hold over God and God doesn't allow Satan to punish Job because he has sinned. Neither has God permitted Job's suffering to authenticate his faith. There is a deeper truth here. The suffering of the righteous has much more to do with grace and the love of God for his people than of anyone having to prove anything to him – or to Satan. God loves Job, and he loves you, even as he loves his one and only Son, the Lord Jesus. That's the truth we need to unpick as we explore Job's story.

1.   Moberley, RWL (2013) Old Testament Theology: Reading the Hebrew Bible as Christian Scripture. Baker Academic Grand Rapids Michigan, 248

CHAPTER 3

What I feared (Job 2:11-3:26)

In some respects the opening two chapters of Job read like a newspaper article reporting on the demise of some wealthy business tycoon. We can sympathise with his story, but it seems a million miles away from the world we inhabit. Yet in chapter 3 everything changes, for here we have a pure cry for help from someone who has lost everything and it matters not whether that person is rich or poor, young or old, man or woman, Jew or Gentile. We can all identify with the anguish of this man. Suffering is a great leveller. It leaves us naked; it strips away all our defences, exposes our vulnerability and fills us with dread. As Job himself cries out in verse 25 *'What I feared has come upon me; what I dreaded has happened to me.'*

What are you afraid of? I don't mean are you scared of spiders, birds or public speaking, nor even do you suffer from a condition like agoraphobia or vertigo. I mean, what is your deepest fear? The one from which all other fears and anxieties spring? It often goes unnamed, unspoken, yet it lurks in the depths of our subconscious waiting for its moment to strike - and when it does, it reduces us to some pitiful creature that hugs itself tight in the corner of a room, trembling with fear; inconsolable tears streaming down its face.

Many thought Job would have nothing to fear at all. He was the greatest man among all the people of the East. He owned vast tracts of land and kept thousands of camels and sheep, hundreds of oxen and donkeys. He was enormously wealthy with many servants at his beck at call and he lived, no doubt, in the equivalent of a millionaire's mansion. He was blessed with a loving wife, seven sons and three daughters who were his pride and joy. Job was a good man, an honest, hardworking farmer, a generous employer, a kind-hearted neighbour, a loving husband and father. He was admired and respected by everybody. Of what could he possibly be afraid?

Job's Fear

From his earliest memory, Job had put his trust in the maxim, 'those who obey God will be blessed with divine favour.' Over the years, Job had witnessed this truth confirmed time and time again, until it took root in his heart – and with that he came to worship his God, not simply for his gifts, but for who he was, a gracious and glorious God. So it was that Job loved God as a man might love his king, and he basked in the glory of that relationship. But there lay the source of his greatest fear, that God would one day desert him, for what claim could he ever have on one so holy and glorious. The more successful and happy he became the deeper was his dread. Like a wife who worships her handsome successful husband whilst feeling unworthy of his affection or a son constantly striving to make his father proud, Job lived with the constant fear of God's rejection.

Job did everything he could so as not to offend or give his God any reason for complaint. His fear extended to his wife and children, who did not seem to share his love for God, no matter how much he sought to persuade them and pray for them. They feasted and partied without any apparent concern. He alone offered the sacrifices and prayed earnestly that God would spare them. If God should leave Job, what would become of them? As Job sits on the ash heap scraping his sores with a piece of broken pottery, his fear creeps to the surface, and reduces him to despair. There's no going back. God has abandoned him – the king has found fault with his servant. His children are lost, his body is broken and his hope has gone. All that remains are questions, 'why has God left me? Why does God hate me so much?'

Job's despair

As Job is forced to confront his fear he begins to question his very existence – and the conclusions he reaches are those of a man brought to the brink of despair,

> *'May the day of my birth perish,*
> *and the night it was said, 'A boy is born!'*
> *That day – may it turn to darkness;*
> *may God above not care about it;*
> *may no light shine upon it.*

May darkness and deep shadow claim it once more.
That night – may thick darkness seize it;
may it not be included among the days of the year
nor be entered in any of the months.
May that night be barren;
may no shout of joy be heard in it.
May those who curse days, curse that day…
for it did not shut the doors of the womb on me
to hide trouble from my eyes.'

Job 3:1-10 selected verses

Job wishes that the day of his birth be cursed and removed forever from the divine record, for it has brought forth nothing but unimaginable suffering. It would have been better if he had never been born. All the blessings he had once known, all his previous happiness, all his success and the joy of the family he once had, count for nothing in the face of his relentless distress. Some might say 'better to have loved and lost than never to have loved at all.' That was not Job's feeling. His bitterness cries out from a heart that has been broken into as many pieces as the pottery with which he scrapes himself. There seems no way back for Job and no way forward. Memory of his past makes his present seem all the more unbearable. For Job the day of his birth brings no joy, no hope and no meaning.

I see Job sifting through his photo album ripping out all the pictures that have him in them and throwing them into the ashes. Pictures of him holding his new-born children in his arms; photographs of his wedding day; photos of his graduation, his school days, the celebration of his coming of age. Back further still, he crumples and crushes snaps of him growing up, winning his first race, taking his first step, and gaining his first tooth. Finally, he gets to the day of his birth, sees his mother and father smiling at this small child in their arms. They look so happy: If only they had known the heartache that was to come. I see the tears coursing down his face as he squeezes his fist around the last photograph, as if in so doing he could squeeze the very life out of his soul.

Job's lament

In his anguish, Job continues to lament, expressing his wish that he had perished at birth for at least he would be now at peace with the kings of the earth,

> *'Why did I not perish at birth, and die as I came*
>   *from the womb?*
> *For now I would be lying down in peace;*
> *I would be asleep and at rest with the kings and*
>   *counsellors of the earth.'*
>   Job 3:11-14 selected verses

Those facing death will often look back on their lives, as if to validate their existence or rehearse their plea at the pearly gates. Many will make confession or seek assurance of a good life. Job had hoped to live out his days and come to death without a blot on his copybook. Now, he faces shame and disgrace. He would rather have died at birth and be at peace rather than face the very real prospect of dying under God's eternal displeasure. In a final outburst of despair, Job questions the purpose of life if it leads only to misery;

> *'Why is light given to those in misery and life to the*
>   *bitter of soul,*
> *to those who long for death that does not come,*

> *who search for it more than for hidden treasure…*
> *why is life given to man whose way is hidden,*
> *whom God has hedged in?'* Job 3:20-23

Why does God prolong the life of those in misery, who want simply to die? Why does God keep alive those who can see no future for their life and no joy in their present? Job feels constrained to walk a dark, fearful path with no prospect of salvation. He feels much like the little match girl looking in through the window at a happy family enjoying Christmas, whilst she freezes and fades away outside. Nobody cares, nobody sees, least of all God!

You are not alone

In these few short verses Job has laid bear his soul before his friends and God, cursing the day of his birth and expressing his longing for death. Who of us has not at one time been caused to reflect on the meaning of our lives during a time of severe trial? Who of us has not been terrified with the thought of God's anger? Who of us has wondered if we will ever be happy again? Who has not prayed with the psalmist,

> *'How long, O Lord? Will you forget me forever?*
> *How long will you hide your face from me?*
> *How long must I wrestle with my thoughts*
> *and every day have sorrow in my heart?'*
> Psalm 13:1-2a

Job's lament reminds us that we are not alone, for in him we have one who has shared in our suffering, who understands our despair and who knows our deepest fear. Job's story is our story; we have an affinity with him and our hope is to be found in his redemption. Furthermore, Job points us to the Lord Jesus who experienced the horror of the cross alone, deserted by his closest disciples and forsaken by his heavenly Father, crying from the cross, *'My God, My God, why have you forsaken me.'* (Matthew 27:46). There lies our hope, for if we can find our story within those of Job and Jesus then we too will find our redemption and the answers we seek, for it was at their lowest point that God raised them up and glorified them.

Cry out to God

For the present, as we experience Job's anguish, we learn that it's ok to be upset and express anger towards God - He can take it. We must not underestimate the courage it would have taken Job to pour out his heart, express his doubts and voice his complaint. Job was highly regarded in the community for his piety, his morality and above all his steadfast faith in God. For him to speak out so openly of his fears and doubts is an indication of the desperation he felt. Often, we can feel as though we are letting God down by complaining about our situation. We tell ourselves our faith is weak if we express anger and doubt, but authentic Christianity is not stoicism; it is not an impassive submission to a set of doctrinal statements. Genuine faith is a personal living relationship with God – and I cannot think of any worthwhile relationship that doesn't involve the heart as well as the mind (Mark 12:30; Romans 10:9,10)!

If you are experiencing great anguish at this time and, like Job, feel you need to scream at God – then do it! To suppress your pain and lock away your feelings will leave you miserable and create a root of bitterness that will erode your hope in God.

Listen to the bitterness of Jeremiah (Jeremiah 20:14-18), in words so like Job's, and his cries in Lamentations 3:1-18, that you might know that in your suffering you are walking in the footsteps of giants, men of tremendous faith and courage. Pour out your heart to God for he will not rebuke your honesty, and join your pleas for help with the prayers of godly people who, down the ages, have tirelessly beseeched God for justice and mercy – and found in him their salvation. Put your arguments to the Lord, reminding him of his commitment to save all who put their hope in him and his exhortation to 'ask and it shall be given to you; seek and you shall find; knock and the door will be opened (Matthew 7:7).' Plead with him that it is to his glory that he delivers you, for it is those who are lifted up who praise their Saviour, not those who go down to the depths. Cry out to him, even if you do not know how to put your distress into words. A mother will not turn away from her baby because he is unable to explain his need. His simple cry is enough to send her running straight away to his side. Even so, your heavenly Father will rush to help you. Remember how Jacob wrestled all night with the angel and refused to let him go until he received a blessing (Genesis 22:22-32)! Remember the parable of the persistent widow (Luke 18:1-8) and our Lord's encouragement not to give up but to keep praying earnestly with faith. In all your suffering, be prepared to wrestle with God to obtain the blessing you so desperately need.

Look to Jesus

Finally, in your suffering look to Jesus for not only has he shared our story (Isaiah 53:3), but also he came specifically to shoulder our burdens (Matthew 11:28) and pay the price of our sin. Satan will whisper in your ear that you have been forsaken, that God will have no more to do with you and that you have no hope of salvation. Yet, your response must always be that you come before God not in your own righteousness but in and through the righteousness of Christ (Romans 5:1). Be assured, that even now, in the midst of your suffering, the Lord is with you and will never forsake you. He intercedes for you before the throne of God with his wounded hands outstretched to the Father. He suffered and died for you, and he will not leave his task of bringing you to the Father unfinished by failing to plead your cause. As the apostle Paul declares,

> *'Who shall separate us from the love of Christ? Shall trouble or hardship or persecution or famine or nakedness or danger or sword? As it is written: 'For your sake we face death all day long; we are considered as sheep to be slaughtered.' No, in all these things we are more than conquerors through him who loved us'*   Romans 8:34b-37

There is much more to say about this but first we must listen to the advice given by Job's friends as emissaries of the world's wisdom!

CHAPTER 4

Friends like us (Job 4:1-5:27, 8:1-22; 11:1-20)

The day Elsie died, Joan lost her soul mate of 72 years. They had been best friends since primary school and shared everything together: Even their husbands had been twin brothers. Joan had never needed to explain what she was feeling or justify her actions, for Elsie understood her better than she herself. They had lived, loved, made mistakes, laughed and wept together and now she was gone. How was she ever to face another day without her friend?

Where would we be without friends? 'A friend in need is a friend indeed,' is a popular maxim, and certainly during periods of great physical and emotional trial we all need friends to comfort and sustain us. As we consider the responses of Job's friends it is helpful to ask ourselves two questions. Firstly, whom can we rely on for support and wise counsel? Secondly, how can we become those able to minister pastorally and spiritually to those in need?

In the last chapter we left Job sitting among the ashes, scrapping himself with fragments of pottery, a portrait of misery and despair. His world has come crashing down and he is at a loss to know why. He is trapped in a nightmare from which he knows no escape for his greatest fear has been realised – God has abandoned him. His friends come to visit and they cannot believe their eyes. He is barely recognisable as the man they once knew and in their distress at seeing him, these three grown men simply burst into tears. For days they sit alongside him, saying nothing, for there is nothing they can say. Finally, Job begins to pour out his heart to them and what they hear shocks them to the core. Job was ever the optimist, always the one who knew what to do and always the encourager, but who was this man they were hearing, who now curses the day of his birth and wishes he had never been born? Who was this man who cries out that he simply wants to die? It is to this outburst that Job's friends feel they simply must respond – but how? How does anyone minister to someone in the pit of despair?

Eliphaz

Eliphaz seems to be the acknowledged leader of the group, and of all Job's friends he is perhaps the gentlest and the most deeply moved by Job's demeanour. Yet from the outset it is clear that he has no understanding of Job's pain and grief. Indeed, how can he, for he has neither lost his entire family within one day, nor been plagued with sores from head to toe; neither still has he ever felt utterly forsaken by his God. Despite this, he begins by saying, *'if someone ventures a word with you, will you be impatient?'* (4:2). Eliphaz has something to say and he thinks Job will not receive his words easily, so he urges patience on Job's part, to hear him out and give weight to his advice. It may seem as if Eliphaz has got it all worked out, like some smug counsellor, easing back in his comfy chair and addressing a client with a problem he has dealt with so many times before. It's more likely, however, that he is so emotionally affected by what he sees that he has to withdraw and remain a little detached. He retreats behind the accepted wisdom usually given to someone who is grieving, for he fears being sucked into Job's despair. Eliphaz may sound assured but in actual fact he is totally in the dark and unable to relate to the depth of Job's pain.

Arguably, the most difficult part of ministering to others is allowing our own barriers to fall, so that we may enter into their suffering, for in so doing it brings to the surface our own doubts and fears. This Eliphaz is unwilling to do. Instead, he begins by trying to get Job to focus on the positives, his godly character and respect, rather than his grief, suffering and humiliation. He reminds Job of the many occasions he has helped others in the past through their times of distress,

> *'Think how you have instructed many,*
> *how you have strengthened feeble hands.*
> *Your words have supported those who stumbled;*
> *you have strengthened faltering knees.*
> *But now trouble comes to you, and you are*
>   *discouraged;*
> *it strikes you and you are dismayed.*
> *Should not your piety be your confidence*
> *and your blameless ways your hope?'*   Job 4:3-6

Pick yourself up

Probably without meaning to, Eliphaz is inferring that Job's suffering is no different to what countless others have experienced and come through; indeed he has supported and encouraged them through such times. Consequently, he should take his own advice, pick himself up and put his trust in his own religious piety and moral goodness. Eliphaz is trying to be reassuring whilst not getting involved. Rather than encouraging Job to continue to speak about his grief and promising to listen and share his journey, he calls upon Job to be his own support and to put his trust in his own respectability. Eliphaz doesn't want to be drawn, for he prefers to remain in the comfort of his own ideology. He blinds himself to Job's situation and argues *'who, being innocent, has ever perished? Where were the upright ever destroyed?'* (4:7) - The answer is in fact right before his eyes – Job! Undeterred, Eliphaz goes on to affirm that it is his belief that it is not the innocent, but those who plough evil and sow trouble that reap it (4:8). His implication is that Job has nothing to worry about. His suffering is merely a storm in a teacup! As Eliphaz holds back from sharing in Job's distress, his advice becomes more and more trite and unfeeling.

By way of an explanation of Job's suffering, Eliphaz resorts to mysticism, adding a sense of mystery and wisdom to what is really a very obvious assertion that no one can be more righteous than God (4:12-21). The upshot of this wondrous revelation is Job must accept all people make mistakes, even the most righteous. Job should not complain or be resentful, but accept that *'man is born to trouble as surely as sparks fly upward'* (5:7). Sin and suffering are in our nature: As children cannot help getting dirty, so no one can go through life without a blemish or a cut. 'Boys will be boys,' and life is full of knocks and scrapes. Job should simply accept his failure, bear his hardship, stop mourning and make his appeal to God (5:8).

Eliphaz does not doubt Job's goodness or his devotion to God, but confronted with his misery, he must conclude that Job has committed some misdemeanour. However, God is holy and just, and he will restore Job when he has learned from his punishment. If Job accepts God's discipline he will come forth all the stronger for

> *'blessed is the man who God corrects;*
> *so do not despise the discipline of the Almighty.*
> *For he wounds, but he also binds up;*
> *he injures, but his hands also heal'*   Job 5:17,18

Eliphaz fails to appreciate the seriousness of Job's predicament and completely misapplies God's word by asserting the wretchedness Job is experiencing is purely a result of God correcting his behaviour. God does indeed discipline his children for their good (Hebrews 12:5-12), but how is it possible that anyone, let alone someone as righteous as Job should receive such stern discipline? Job is not complaining about hardship, but the total destruction of his life!

Eliphaz has withdrawn so far from Job's torment, it's as if he sees Job as a test case. I recall many years ago attending a medical conference on the treatment of arthritis and listening to researchers discussing some of the extreme cases presented to them. As they showed images of patients with chronic conditions, exhibiting grossly distorted hands and feet, severe calcification of joints and sub-dermal skin lesions, little mention was made of the intense suffering these people must be experiencing day after day. For the purposes of the presentations, the main focus was on scientific objectivity. In the same way, Eliphaz has made a clinical assessment of Job's pain suggesting it is common experience and soon to be remedied. Furthermore, he shows complete insensitivity asserting that after Job has been disciplined,

> *'you will know your tent is secure;*
> *you will take stock of your property and find nothing*
> *   is missing.*
> *You will know that your children will be many,*
> *and your descendants like the grass of the earth.*
> *You will come to the grave in full vigour,*
> *like sheaves gathered in season.*
> *We have examined this, and it is true.*
> *So hear it and apply it to yourself'*   Job 4:24-27

For a man who has seen all his wealth and property taken away, witnessed the death of all his children and whose body is covered with sores, these words are like salt rubbed harshly into an open wound. How can his situation ever be restored? How can anyone possibly think that his experience is but a passing phase? How can anyone seriously believe that such suffering is merely a form of discipline?

Bildad

If Eliphaz has been gentle in broaching the issue of Job's suffering and grief, Bildad shows no such restraint as he delivers his opening salvo. Bildad, the traditionalist, is passionate for God's justice and is insistent that whatever Job may think or say, however much he may weep and wail, God's punishment is for a reason. However nicely one may try to package the truth, Job or a member of his family has clearly committed a sin! This cannot be ignored and the only recourse is for Job to repent. Bildad begins his assault on Job, for that is surely what it is, with some very insensitive words considering Job's bereavement and lament in chapter 3,

> *'Does God pervert justice?*
> *Does the Almighty pervert what is right?*
> *When your children sinned against him,*
> *he gave them over to the penalty of their sin'*
>
> Job 8:3, 4

Job's seven sons and three daughters were the apple of his eye and the light of his life. They were a close family who often met and celebrated together. Job would continually pray for them and sacrifice burnt offerings in case they inadvertently sinned against God. His over-riding desire was that they would each come to know the Lord and worship him. Bildad is asserting that the mighty wind that struck the house where they were feasting, killing them all, was not a tragic accident but the judgement of God. They had sinned and the Almighty was not prepared to accept Job's sacrifices for them any longer. They had reaped the whirlwind and consequently were no better than the ungodly that do not know God. Their fate was akin to that of Nadab and Abihu whom God put to death for offering unauthorised fire before the Lord (Leviticus 10:1-7). Just as their father Aaron was not to grieve but accept the judgement of God, so too, Bildad argues, Job should acknowledge his guilt and move on. It's hard to imagine harsher words. Within a few short sentences, Bildad has tarnished the lives of Job's children, questioned Job's parenting skills, trashed Job's religious zeal and damned all Job's prayers for his children's salvation. Bildad burdens Job with the guilt that he should have done more as a parent to protect his children. If this is not enough, Bildad proceeds to question Job's own standing before God as a blameless, godly man, hinting at so much with that simple word, 'if',

> *'if you will look to God and plead with the Almighty,*
> *if you are pure and upright,*
> *even now he will rouse himself on your behalf*
> *and restore you to your rightful place.'*   Job 8:5, 6

Whereas Eliphaz encouraged Job to put his trust in his piety and blameless ways, Bildad brings them into question, querying Job's moral integrity. He appeals to the wisdom of former generations, concerning the destiny of those who forget God, arguing that as plants wither and perish when cut off or ripped away from their source, so those who forget God will surely perish (8:8-19). He tries to reassure Job that God will restore him and grant him happiness once more, but the damage has been done. Job does indeed feels as though he has been ripped out of the soil and cut off from the source of all joy and happiness. Bildad's words, far from bringing comfort, give him even more reason to despair.

Zophar

Zophar, arguably the most blunt and outspoken of the three friends, takes a very pragmatic view, openly accusing Job of sin,

> *'You say to God, 'My beliefs are flawless and I am*
> *   pure in your sight.'*
> *Oh, how I wish that God would speak,*

that he would open his lips against you
and disclose to you the secrets of true wisdom…
Know this: God has even forgotten some of your sin'

Job 11:4-6

For him, the remedy is obvious,

'if you devote your heart to him and stretch out your
hands to him,
if you put away the sin that is in your hand
and allow no evil to dwell in your tent;
then you will lift up your face without shame;
you will stand firm and without fear'

Job 11:13-15

According to Zophar, Job needs to return to God, repent of his sin and God will restore him once more! Indeed, it will be as if it had never happened, like water flowing under the bridge. Zophar paints a wonderful picture of how it will be, saying that Job will never know darkness again, he will always feel secure and have hope, no-one will make him afraid and he will be as popular and sought after as ever he was before his sudden disgrace (11:17-19). There are people in this world for whom everything is black and white. Every situation should be approached with the same merciless logic and any suggestion of sentiment stamped out as it only serves to cloud judgement and muddy the water. Zophar is just such a person whose faith is purely intellectual and for whom a relationship with God could be defined as 'it's business, not personal.' The problem for Job, however, is that his suffering is all too personal. He feels he is under God's wrath and God is attacking him as a thug would beat an innocent victim lying on the ground. It is his property that has been stolen, his family that has been murdered, and his health that has been taken from him. To argue that the one doing it will simply stop and everything will be all right again if Job should simply say sorry is nonsense!

Job's friends have approached Job with the sincere intention of comforting and supporting him through this most difficult time of his life. For days they have sat with him in silence, appalled at his suffering, and they have wept with him. How much we have valued friends such as these who have not tried to breeze in and cheer us up with empty words and gestures. How often what we most need are those who do not pass judgement but pledge their silent support! Eliphaz, Bildad and Zophar were just such friends who were prepared to visit Job even when his family stayed away. However, it appears that they simply could not handle the intensity of Job's suffering and as we will see they had no theological framework to address his situation. Consequently, their attempts to encourage Job were woefully inadequate; their words only served to deepen Job's anguish. Eliphaz reduced his torment to God's discipline; Bildad regarded it as a reprimand for his children's transgressions and Zophar as chastisement for Job's sin against God. All insist his suffering is only explicable because of sin and easily remedied by repentance. In so doing they not only belittle their friend but also destroy any hope he may have of restoration. As people committed to his welfare they have failed miserably and it is important for us to understand why, so that we too do not make the same mistakes, and hurt those we wish to heal.

An Inadequate Theology of Suffering

Suffering is an enigma; like trying to piece together a jigsaw puzzle with no picture. When my children begin a jigsaw puzzle they rarely search out the edges and corners first. Instead they find the pieces that make up a character they recognise and try to build out from there. They start with what they know as their basis for moving out into the unknown. Job's friends do the same when it comes to understanding suffering. They begin with two pieces of incontrovertible truth about God and morality. Firstly, God is holy and righteous, incapable of injustice and without partiality. Secondly, they take as axiomatic that we live in a moral world where everybody gets what he or she deserves. The good will be rewarded and the wicked punished, for 'a man reaps what he sows.' It is at this point that his friends distort this axiom, for they go on to assert that if a person suffers it must therefore be because of something they have done. For Job's friends the question 'why do bad things happen to good people?' is a non-question, for it cannot happen. Everything that happens to a person must without exception be his or her own fault.

They do not question the whys or wherefores; they do not doubt the severity of God's punishment fits the crime; they do not ask why some are punished while others go free. It is all in God's hands and God is holy, righteous and just! In the past Christian religious leaders have acted similarly, publicly stating that the parents of African children, who had lost their lives through AIDS, had brought upon themselves the judgement of God. Others have quietly voiced the opinion that some natural disasters are in fact a sign of God's judgement on a nation. Such statements demonstrate how, by inadvertently misapplying a moral principle, one can produce a distorted and heartless theology of suffering that often caricatures the Christian faith. This is Job's difficulty for his friends unequivocally declare him guilty, in the same way that Jesus' disciples attribute sin to the blind man or his parents (John 9:2). Taken to its extreme this view would assert that the woman who is raped is as guilty as her rapist, and the child who is abused as culpable as his abuser.

If we wish to seriously support and encourage those who are suffering we need to get our theology of suffering right. Whilst we live in a moral universe, we must never forget that God is a God of grace and mercy, as well as justice and holiness. Time and again the holy scriptures present God as one who grieves the loss of even a single life, who cares for the sparrow and numbers the hairs on our heads; a God who is unwilling that any should perish, but desires everyone to come to repentance (1 Peter 3:9); a Lord who does not condemn the woman caught in adultery (John 8:11), who delivers those possessed by demons (Mark 5:1-20) and who prays for forgiveness for those who would crucify him on the cross (Luke 23:34). Furthermore, we need to understand that we live in a broken world in which we cannot so easily separate out the sin from the devastation and suffering it causes. Often there are no elegant solutions to our problems that involve no pain or hurt; every choice we make has a downside as well as an up. The best we can ever do is to choose the path that God lays out for us – and that will not necessarily be pain-free. Just as a vaccination can be painful at the time but in the long run be beneficial, so God often needs to take us through situations that are painful, not as discipline, not as punishment but purely for our protection. We need to keep at the forefront of all our thinking that God is love and that he constantly, moment by moment, reaches out to us in love and mercy even though we are estranged from him and under judgement. If we are to produce a credible and comprehensive theology of suffering, we must widen our understanding and listen hard to all Job is trying to tell us.

A distorted view of Job

Job's friends not only have an inadequate theology of suffering, they have allowed their poor moral understanding to colour their relationship with Job. They cannot bear to listen to his rants against God. Before they realise, they have ceased taking any notice of Job's protestations of innocence, even to the point of denying everything they know about his character and goodness. They have stopped seeing him as he truly is, respected, faithful, pious and godly; they see only a destitute, broken and besieged beggar plagued by pain and doubt. They have come to regard his claims for innocence and justice as they would a vagrant's, with disdain and disrespect. Whereas initially they pitied him, they now become frustrated with him, because of his reluctance to repent. Despite all their encouragement and advice he seems determined to lock himself away in his own world of woe.

Maybe you have experienced those who through grief are seemingly unable to move forward. You have visited them day after day, ran errands and helped with household tasks; you have sat with them and prayed for them; you have taken them out and encouraged them to take up new hobbies, but all to no avail. Perhaps you even got to the point where you dreaded going round because you came away so drained. In such situations it is all too easy to become upset and even irritated at their reluctance to make an effort. It is all too easy to see them as the authors of their own demise, but to do so is to miss an opportunity to minister effectively in their lives.

A wrong view of themselves

Job's friends presume that those whose lives are blessed must be without sin. For if suffering is the sign of God's punishment of sin, then the opposite must also be true - if my life is good then God is pleased with me. Not only do they see Job as a beggar, but they see themselves as elevated in his presence. They remonstrate with him, believing they have the moral high ground. They have so distanced themselves from his torment that they fail to recognise they necessarily lie under the same judgement. Yet, Job believed he had done everything he possibly could to remain in God's favour. He was without equal in the world, blameless and God fearing. If Job was not spared suffering because of his moral goodness, what right has his friends or indeed anyone to expect an untroubled life (Proverbs 11:31)? This understanding that brings us back to our central problem of living spiritually in the East, estranged from God.

It is his friends' misplaced self-confidence that causes them to be so self-righteous and damning toward Job. We get a similar response from the Pharisees and religious leaders when they brought out a woman caught in adultery to test Jesus (John 8:1-10). They could not see that before God they were no better (Romans 3:23). In fact the Pharisees' belief in their own righteousness made them careless about their own walk with God, devoting themselves to ritualistic observance whilst ignoring justice, mercy and faithfulness, for which Jesus rebuked them harshly (Matthew 23:23,24). For those who use their piety to criticise others, pronouncing judgement from ivory towers, Jesus words are a salutary reminder,

'Do not judge or you too will be judged.
For in the same way as you judge others, you will
be judged,
and with the measure you use, it will be measured
to you'   Matthew 7:1, 2

Being a comforter

Job's friends were sincere in seeking to comfort Job. However, they ultimately fail because they have not personally wrestled with their own demons; they simply pass on, without question, the accepted dogma passed down to them. Their reticence to get involved, their inadequate theology and poor opinion of him mean they could do little to minister to his needs. It is hard to condemn them because many of us may have done exactly the same. We want to have simple answers to life's struggles and we don't like getting too involved because it is too emotionally demanding. But if these are our goals then we are not about Christian ministry, for the Lord calls us to take up our cross and follow him. If we want to truly minister to those in need, we must to be prepared to make ourselves vulnerable and be willing to enter into their pain, their doubts and their fear. We need to be ready to listen and to take them seriously and not make quick judgements based on personal prejudice. We need to remember our Lord's words to his disciples,

'Blessed are the poor in spirit, for theirs is the
kingdom of heaven.
Blessed are those who mourn for they will be comforted.
Blessed are the meek for they will inherit the earth.
Blessed are those who hunger and thirst for
righteousness for they will be filled'
Matthew 5:3-6

If we are to become those who minister pastorally and spiritually to others we must take time to ensure we have a prayerful, biblical understanding of suffering that emphasises not only the justice but also the grace, mercy and love of God. When speaking with those facing trials, we must not presume to know their problem or to have all the answers, but rather we must be ready to humbly go together with them to the throne of grace acknowledging our own insufficiency and need. As we sit at the side of those who are poor in spirit, mourning, humbled and thirsting for righteousness, we must above all see them through the eyes of God, who is waiting to bless them and has called us to be a part of their restoration. We should regard our calling to this ministry as a privilege, and be prepared, as our Lord, to humble ourselves that we too may be raised up with them.

Job is just such a friend whom we are, perhaps, just getting to know. We see him in the faces of those around us, at church, at home and at work. He has a story to tell and he wants us to walk with him through the uncertainty. As we journey with him, we will need to lower our own barriers and take the plank out of our own eyes, so that we will see and hear more clearly what the Lord has to say to him. Only then will we become people who can minister graciously to those around us.

CHAPTER 5

Someone to speak for me
(Job 6:1-7:21; 9:1-10:22)

Tom arrived home to find all his possessions piled on the street and the locks changed. He banged repeatedly on the door shouting for Clare, till the neighbours began to twitch the curtains. He got no response. He called but no one picked up; finally he left a text, 'Clare, what's going on? What have I done?' They'd been happily married for almost 12 years, at least that's what he thought. He played back in his mind all the events of the past few days. Nothing. They; he had done everything the same as always. Perhaps that was the problem. She'd said she loved his predictability, but maybe that was a lie. Was it all a lie? Had he mistaken tolerance for love? He tried ringing again but the receiver hung up.

Job feels abandoned

His friends feel Job is whining over his lot, when the solution is perfectly clear; he should repent and turn back to God. However, they fail to appreciate the magnitude of Job's predicament and the depth of his anguish and confusion. For the whole of his life Job has never known a moment when he has not basked in the sunshine of God's love. For Job walking with God has been like living with his best friend, the joy of his life. Every good thing that has happened to Job is because of God and it has been all the more wonderful because it has been shared with God. But now it seems God has inexplicably abandoned him. He cannot understand what he has done wrong, nor why God refuses to answer him.

Those who have experienced broken relationships will understand how Job feels. He is in turmoil. He is lost and broken hearted. Nothing he can do has any value without God. He wants to return to God but he doesn't know how, because he cannot figure out why God has rejected him. His wife has counselled, 'curse God and die' (2:9) and his friends have offered him glib answers that have no real substance. They insist he admit his failure and do the right thing: Eventually God will restore him. He simply needs to move on and not wallow in his grief. But how can he? God's abandonment isn't something he can grit his teeth and endure (6:11-13) for his suffering is such that without God's gracious intervention he can see no way forward. Any hope or meaning he may have in life is inseparable from being with God. He cries out for God to simply take his life that at least he might take consolation in never having denied his Lord (6:10), for this unrelenting torment is more than he can bear. Yet, Job cannot give up either and simply walk away from the greatest joy he has ever known. He needs an opportunity to tell God what he is feeling. He wants to assure the Lord that he would never be deceitful and deny his God, and he wants to say that he feels used and abused (7:1-5). In desperation he pours out his heart to God, pleading for mercy,

> 'My days are swifter than a weaver's shuttle,
>   and they come to an end without hope.
> Remember, O God, that my life is but a breath,
>   my eyes will never see happiness again.
> The eye that now sees me, will see me no longer;
>   you will look for me, but I will be no more.
> As a cloud vanishes and is gone,
>   so he who goes down to the grave does not return.
> He will never come to his house again;
>   his place will know him no more…
>   you will search for me, but I shall be no more'
>   Job 7:6-10, 21b also 9:25-26

Twice over he calls upon the Lord to recognise the fleeting nature of his life, for soon he will be gone and forgotten; without the Lord he will never know happiness again. If the Lord does not come soon, he will be lost forever. Is that what the Lord really wants? Job refuses to believe that! I can imagine Job looking back over the times he has been with the Lord, blessed times in prayer when he felt his soul singing before his heavenly Father; times spent walking through the meadow when such peace came upon him, filling him with joy and praise; times sat with the widow and the dying when the Lord gave him the words to comfort them and they opened their hearts to their saviour. Surely God has delighted in him, just as much as he has found his joy in the Lord: Their relationship could not be a lie.

Yet, as he ponders his situation and God's apparent rejection, he becomes increasingly bitter, despising his life and resenting God's unwelcome scrutiny.

> 'Am I the sea or the monster of the deep, that you put
>   me under guard?
> When I think my bed will comfort me and my couch
>   will ease my complaint,
> even then you frighten me with dreams and terrify
>   me with visions,
> so that I prefer strangling and death, rather than
>   this body of mine.
> I despise my life; I would not live for ever.
> Let me alone; my days have no meaning'
>
> Job 7:12-16

Job resents God's attentiveness

Job is in a desperate place. In his earlier life he enjoyed God's continued presence and delighted in God's attentiveness, like a wife delights in her husband or a child in his mother. Like the psalmist he might well have sung,

> 'when I consider your heavens, the work of your
> fingers, the moon and the stars, which you have set
> in place, what is man that you are mindful of him,
> the son of man that you care for him? You made him
> a little lower than the heavenly beings and crowned
> him with glory and honour'   Psalm 8:3-5

Every day he and God walked together and opened their hearts to each other, Job delightfully sharing every detail of his life with his God. But now, he dreads God's intimate knowledge of him and fears his examination, which now feels more like a divorce lawyer picking over the details his life to uncover some indiscretion. In his distress he resents God's attention, feeling as he draws near to death that he simply wants to be left alone to die in peace. His only response is to question God's scrutiny of his life,

> 'What is man that you make so much of him,
>> that you give him so much attention,
>> that you examine him every morning and test
>> him every moment?
> Will you never look away from me, or let me alone
>> even for an instant?
> If I have sinned, what have I done to you, O watcher
>> of men?
> Why have you made me your target? Have I become
>> a burden to you?
> Why do you not pardon my offences and forgive my
>> sins?'   Job 7:17-21a

Job is not like Almighty God, eternal, holy and without sin; he is mortal and imperfect. He knows this and God surely knows this, so why does God not make allowances for his humanity? What more could Job have done to prove his love for God? Why must God examine him every morning, seeking out the smallest of imperfections, so that he can drive them out with the rod of affliction? Job is struggling to understand how a God who for most of his life has been so attentive and loving, can suddenly cast him aside without any thought and subject him to such misery.

How to approach God?

Some people have very exacting standards. Just being around them is scary; you can feel as though they are watching every little thing you do, waiting to point out a mistake or to let you know how you should improve. Sometimes, we might question why they take such an avid interest in us and the things we are doing. We might even try to avoid them because they make us feel so uncomfortable. Even in our deeper relationships we may want to withhold from our partners something we have done, because we feel they would disapprove or want to know all the details. When questioned we may try to change the subject or evade the issue in some way. Job is not like that for he longs to be restored in his communion with the Lord. He dreads God's examination of his life, but he doesn't want to avoid God; he wants to bring his case before him. But here lies Job's dilemma. God is too pure, too profound and too incomprehensible to approach,

> 'He moves mountains without their knowing it and
>> overturns them in his anger.
> He shakes the earth from its place and makes its
>> pillars tremble.
> He speaks to the sun and it does not shine; he seals
>> off the light of the stars.
> He alone stretches out the heavens and treads on the
>> waves of the sea.
> He is the Maker of the Bear and Orion, the Pleiades
>> and the constellations of the south.
> He performs wonders that cannot be fathomed,
>> miracles that cannot be counted'   Job 9:5-10

Job is in awe of God and even though he feels God's rejection acutely and questions his mistreatment, he cannot help but worship and adore him. Job has never believed himself worthy of God's love. He has always regarded himself as the one truly blessed by the relationship for what is he before the Almighty. God is altogether glorious, more radiant than the most brilliant star, more pure than a flawless diamond, more weighty than gold; whose justice stands higher than the mountains and whose love extends farther than the horizon. By contrast Job is a mere man, limited in every way. He has never questioned God before about anything. It would be churlish and arrogant to dispute with the mighty and Eternal One, the King of kings and Lord of lords, for Job is but dust and ashes. How can a beggar summon a king? Furthermore, in their present antagonism why should God even consider granting him a hearing? He would rightly crush him and reduce him to nothing (9:16-18). As soon as he opened his mouth to speak, Job would condemn himself (9:20). Martin Luther expresses the same sentiment prior to his conversion,

> *'Who am I, that I should lift up mine eyes or raise my hands to the divine Majesty? The angels surround him. At his nod the earth trembles. And shall I, a miserable little pygmy, say 'I want this, I ask for that?' For I am dust and ashes and full of sin and I am speaking to the living, Eternal and the true God'* [1]

God shows no favouritism

Job's only recourse is to examine the nature of God's relationship with humanity, striving to resolve what he feels are inconsistencies in the way justice is dispensed by God (9:21-24). For the first time he begins to see himself, through God's eyes, as one who dwells among the people of the East, separated from the covenant promises of God. He is just a man amongst men, living outside of the kingdom of God; one who is but a potsherd among the potsherds on the ground (Isaiah 45:9). Whilst his friends may despise him for his piteous state, now he begins to loathe himself – for even when he was at his best, what was he to God that he should be singled out for his favour? Before the glory and perfection of God, of what value is his moral goodness? Though a man should the best that ever was still he would be but a stain upon God's robe. Even the most glorious deed done by the godliest person would be to God's goodness, like a dark spot on the surface of the Sun. Outside of God's covenantal grace, all are equal and all are equally lost. Job concludes that it is for this reason that God does not show partiality between the good and the wicked, since before him they are all alike under the judgement. Therefore God

> 'destroys both the blameless and the wicked.'
> When a scourge brings sudden death,
> he mocks the despair of the innocent.
> When a land falls into the hands of the wicked,
> he blindfolds its judges. If it is not he, then, who is
> it?'   Job 9:22-24;12:21.

Job is not questioning God's right to do as he pleases, but he is beginning to realise that if it is a matter of justice, as his friends so convincingly argue, then all people are equally condemned, whether good or bad, before the holiness and purity of God. We all live outside of Eden and are judged purely on the basis of our own righteousness, and there is no-one good enough to stand before God in his majesty. This is quite an unpalatable thought for it takes away any reliance anyone may have on moral goodness. Job and his friends, like so many others, have always believed that the 'good go to heaven,' but this is not the conclusion Job is coming to as he wrestles with his suffering. Until now he has never thought to question what happens to the innocent and the wicked, but now his eyes are opened and he realises that all equally suffer and die. There is no difference – God does not discriminate. As he considers the world he sees that the innocent child cradled in his mother's arms is no more spared pain and suffering in this life than the hardened criminal on death row. From this he inevitably concludes that all our righteousness and moral goodness count for nothing in terms of our being able to approach the Holy One! How then can Job win an audience and be reconciled to God?

Someone to arbitrate

As Job considers the hopelessness of his situation, perhaps he thinks back to Lot, a righteous man living among the people of Sodom and Gomorrah (2 Peter 2:6-8). Due to their flagrant sin and disobedience, God had determined to destroy the city and all its inhabitants. Yet, Abraham, a man in a covenantal relationship with God (Genesis 15:1-6), had spoken with the Almighty pleading on behalf of the city (Genesis 18:16-33), and through his mediation Lot and his children were spared. If only, Job supposes, he had a mediator or advocate to plead his cause before the throne,

> 'someone to arbitrate between us, to lay his hand
> upon us both,
> someone to remove God's rod from me

> *so that his terror would frighten me no more*
> *then I would speak up without fear'*   Job 9:33,34

This is an amazing leap of faith by a man who is in the pit of despair. Faced with the prospect of eternal separation and destruction, he cries out for someone to represent him before Almighty God. Perhaps he's reminded of righteous Mordecai, who learning of Haman's plot to destroy the Jews, went to his cousin Esther. Mordecai knew he would have no chance of bringing his petition to King Xerxes, *'for any man or woman who approaches the king in the inner court without being summoned, the king has but one law: that he be put to death'* (Esther 4:11). Yet, his cousin Esther was queen and therefore had great influence with the king. Mordecai persuaded Esther and through her intervention the people were spared. In the same way, Job realises he needs a mediator of sufficient worth to come before Almighty God, someone of purer life, willing to listen to Job and uphold his complaint.

A Lifeline

As Job considers the possibility of a mediator, he falls into prayer recounting what he should say if he were granted an audience with Almighty God. Job marshals his arguments appealing to God's justice and loving kindness, before calling upon God to realise the sternness and severity of his punishment. He begins by pleading with the Lord to spare him and to inform him of his offence. He begs God not to judge him so harshly whilst seeming to look casually upon the sins of the wicked. He asks for his integrity to recognised and queries the Lord's need to search out all his indiscretions,

> *'Do not condemn me, but tell me what charges you*
> *have against me.*
> *Does it please you to oppress me, to spurn the work*
> *of your hands, while you smile on the schemes of the*
> *wicked? Do you have eyes of flesh?*
> *Do you see as a mortal sees?*
> *Are your days like those of a mortal or your years like*
> *those of a man, that you must search out my faults*
> *and probe after my sin – though you know that I am*
> *not guilty and that no one can rescue me from your*
> *hand?'* Job 10:2-7

He continues his plea, contemplating his own conception and birth, which earlier he had wished never happened. Like the psalmist, he is filled with awe as he meditates on God spending weeks, patiently and lovingly, bending over his tiny form, joining his bones together attaching muscle and sinew (Psalm 139:1-16). He imagines God fashioning his heart and creating the millions upon millions of blood vessels; he envisages God smiling as the heart begins to beat, pumping the blood around his body, bringing life to each and every organ. He marvels at God clothing him with skin and applying those little finishing touches that made him so unique. He reminds the Lord that he created and moulded him in his image - surely God truly loved Job then,

> *'Your hands shaped me and made me.*
> *Will you now turn and destroy me?*
> *Remember that you moulded me like clay.*
> *Will you now turn me to dust again?*
> *Did you not pour me out like milk and curdle me*
> *like cheese, clothe me with skin and flesh and knit*
> *me together with bones and sinews?*

You gave me life and showed me kindness,
and in your providence watched over my spirit'

Job 10:8-12

Why expect so much of me?

I imagine Job looking back at the photograph of his father cradling him, glowing with pride and smiling with wonder at the tiny life in his arms. His parents were strict for they had great plans for him. They wanted him to grow up to be respected in the community, a man of stature and honour. He had fully accepted their discipline without complaint, even when he felt it undeserved, for he knew they had his best interests at heart and he trusted their wisdom. He accepted that God too would discipline him and he willingly embraced that if only to be all that his God desired. But in bitterness of soul, Job now cries out that he feels God is too strict, demanding too much of his child. From the outset, he insists, God must have intended to punish any offence he might commit no matter how small (10:13,14).

Job feels God is treating him like an uncompromising parent imposing an extremely harsh regime to bring out the very best in their child. He believes God is trying to present him as a model of perfection, which he simply cannot be. He has tried so hard all his life, because he loves God and longs to please him. His joy is in knowing God is proud of him and he will endure anything for a smile – but now Job does not sense God's smile; only his anger and that is what hurts so much. In his musing Job despairs, for even if he is innocent, he feels he cannot lift up his head before God, for he is full of shame and drowned in his affliction (10:15).

Job has so many questions: If God loves him so much and has created him so wonderfully, why has he placed such high expectations upon him that he could never fulfil? How is it to God's glory for people to see him broken and in despair? If this was God's purpose all along, why bless him with his love, why bring him into the world in the first place? As Job struggles to make sense of it all he falls back into gloom, crying out: *'If only I have never come into being, or had been carried straight from the womb to the grave! Turn away from me so that I can have a moment's joy'* (10:19-20).

Jesus is our advocate

Job's hope has briefly flickered like a candle but still he is struggling to make sense of God's purposes. He has arrived at a pivotal point, to which he will return, concerning his need for an advocate, but he is still filled more with questions than answers. What Job could not know, but we do through the revelation of God in Christ, is that God has indeed provided us with a mediator, the Lord Jesus Christ (1 Timothy 2:5). As Job complained, *'do you have eyes of flesh? Do you see as a mortal sees?'* so the Word became flesh and made his dwelling among us (John 1:14). He took upon himself our humanity and carried our sorrows that he might fully know us and be as one of us, even as he is fully God. Jesus has great influence with Almighty God, for he is God's one and only Son, and he has our interests on his heart for he is our brother (Hebrews 2:11,12). In our suffering we can turn to the Lord Jesus to take up our case and make our plea before the throne of God. Jesus is fully able to plead our cause for he is without spot or blemish and through his own blood he has entered into the Holy of Holies that he might be our advocate. Indeed, God himself appointed him to be our high priest in the order of Melchizedek that he may ever live to make intercession for us. As the writer the Hebrews declares,

> *'we do not have a high priest who is unable to sympathise with our weaknesses, but we have one who has been tempted in every way, just as we are – yet was without sin.*
> *Let us then approach the throne of grace with confidence, so that we may receive mercy and find grace to help us in our time of need'*
>
> Hebrews 4:15,16

Marshal your arguments

Since God has provided us with the perfect mediator, Jesus Christ, we can be sure God wants us to come before him and pour out our hearts to him. If there were no hope of restoration, if God saw nothing of value in us, then he would not have provided Jesus. God does not want us to suffer in silence, to grit our teeth and bare it; he wants us to tell him how we feel and to call upon him for justice. Consequently, in supporting others we need to encourage them in prayer to marshal their arguments to present to the Lord. We need to urge them to be clear in their petition, for even though our Lord knows our needs even before we ask, still he desires to hear those needs expressed that it may strengthen our faith in claiming God's promises. We need to prompt them to cry out on the basis that the Lord Jesus knows what it is to suffer. We must enjoin them to pour out their heart to him as one who understands and is full of mercy and loving-kindness, for he is acquainted with all suffering and is willing to bear all our burdens (Isaiah 53:3).

We should entreat them, 'make your case to Almighty God as if to remind him that he created you in love; that his hands shaped and moulded you in the womb. Praise him that he knitted your bones and sinews together, that he clothed you with flesh and that his eyes alone beheld your unformed body. Worship him for he fashioned you as one of a kind; there is no one else like you in the entire world and God has created you for his glory. Tell him that you want to be the person he has called you to be, to walk in his love and to delight in his presence.'

If they should feel God has treated them harshly, encourage them not to suffer in silence but to pour out their complaint to God crying out 'you are filled with shame and you cannot lift your head, unless he should call you into his presence and once more embrace you in his arms of love. Tell him of your love and that you acknowledge that you are nothing before him, but that also you are nothing without him, for he is your life and your hope and your joy.'

If you know someone who is in the midst of despair and doubt, do not wait to take them by the hand and lead them in prayer to the Lord Jesus. As the father brought his demon possessed son (Mark 9:17); as the Samaritan woman invited her neighbours (John 4:29) and as the paralysed man was carried by his friends on a stretcher to Jesus, so we should not hesitate to bring, invite or carry those we care about into the presence of our gracious Lord, for he is merciful and ready to offer salvation to all who come to him in faith. Intercede for them, if they cannot pray for themselves; weep and mourn for their situation and call upon the Lord to make himself known to them. If they are willing, bring them before the elders of the church to pray over and anoint them in the name of the Lord that they may be raised up. Remember the words of James that the prayer of a righteous person is powerful and effective (James 5:13-16).

Jesus laid down his life for us

We all have questions concerning why God should allow us to suffer, but let us not retreat into our despair for God has given to us an advocate, the Lord Jesus Christ, that we may bring our pleas to the throne of grace. Let us not waste a moment in presenting our arguments for the quicker we make our case the more certain we can be of a speedy resolution. The reality is that innocent people suffer; we suffer, and it can seem as if God does not care, or that evil has triumphed. But that is not the case. Though we do not see it as yet and without trying to be trite, God loves us and is desperately concerned about us. Although through the sin of Adam, we are separated from him, yet he cannot stop showering us with blessing. He longs to restore us and to bring us back into his presence and to love us for all eternity. For this reason, he sent his one and only Son to identify with us and take upon himself our infirmities.

In the suffering and death of Christ we see the Righteous One surrendering himself to the hate of Satan. Unlike Job, our Lord Jesus was fully aware of the discussions taking place in the courts of heaven. He understood why he had to suffer and he willingly submitted to death on a cross to bring you and I back to God (1 Peter 3:18). Our Lord had nothing to prove, but he had people that he cared passionately about, you and I (1 John 3:16). In our struggles, we need to hold fast to the truth that Jesus took upon himself the wrath of God and bore it alone on the cross. He broke Satan's claim on us and redeemed us from the effects of sin. If you are suffering unjustly or if you are questioning the power or the love of God for you or even if your situation has caused you to doubt God's existence then know you are in good company. You are not alone and God would not have you be alone. For your sake and for your encouragement he has given you the story of Job. Despite all that he suffered, Job did not yield his faith. I thank God that this is so, because when we face trials, when it is so much easier to deny God and walk away, then we need to stand firm, maintain our integrity and keep faith despite all our doubts, fears and anguish - and Job stands with us. This is a man with whom we can identify, whose faith is not wishy washy nor easily swayed by circumstances. In Job we see a man desperately fighting for his faith, who may have gained a victory but who as yet is still beset with doubt and fear. As we face our struggles, with all our questions, it is good to know that at last we have someone who knows what it means to fight for faith and who will remain steadfast in the fiercest storm.

1.   Bainton, R.H. (1959) Here I Stand: A life of Martin Luther. Mentor books, Abingdon Press. NY p.30

CHAPTER 6

Law and Grace (Job 15:1-35; 18:1-21; 20:1-29)

She was just the bag lady. No one knew how or when she came to live on the streets – no one really cared. Her problems were her own affair and no doubt she had brought her trouble upon herself. She watched them pass by, rushing to and from work, hurrying the children to and from school. All were busy conforming to the law of the jungle - too busy to notice the bag lady, huddled in the doorway, her paltry possessions, barely sheltering her from the elements. Then he stopped and offered her his hand. He spoke gently and helped her up. Taking her bags in one hand and supporting her with the other, he led her into the coffee shop. She sat at a table as he brought her a drink and sandwich. She took his hand softly and with tears in her eyes, whispered, "Thank you, thank you, thank you."

Nobody likes to be labelled, especially when it implies something demeaning. If anything is sure to raise the hackles it is a statement such as 'you are a sinner, a reprobate.' To label someone is to pigeonhole that person; to assert that this is a complete description of all that needs to be known. We use such labels today as, for example, when society identifies a person as a paedophile, an alcoholic, a prostitute or a murderer. Nothing else needs to be said, for that one label apparently communicates all necessary information. Job's friends have been trying to convince Job that he must have sinned in some way, in order to account for his suffering. Since Job refuses to accept their logic, they now proceed to label him as 'wicked, a sinner.' From now on this categorisation colours all their dealings with him, even to the point where Eliphaz later slanders Job's character with unsubstantiated false accusations (22:4-11).

Eliphaz as previously, opens the way by immediately calling Job's wisdom into question, since he continues to insist on his innocence,

> *'Would a wise man answer with empty notions or*
> *fill his belly with the hot east wind?*
> *Would he argue with useless words, with speeches*
> *that have no value?'* Job 15:2,3

Bildad backs up Eliphaz' opinion saying, *'When will you end these speeches? Be sensible, and then we can talk?'* (Job 18:2). For a man who has lost everything and is fighting to hold on to his self-respect, to be told that his words are useless, have no value and are lacking in wisdom, is soul destroying. Job has been the one to whom everyone came for wise council (29:7-10); when he spoke everyone else became silent, out of a deep regard for his learning. But now Eliphaz is supplanting his position, for in his eyes Job is now 'foolish, wicked, a sinner,' and therefore unworthy of respect,

> *'Are you the first man ever born?*
> *Do you listen in on God's council?*
> *Do you limit wisdom to yourself?*
> *What do you know that we do not know?*
> *What insights do you have that we do not have?*
> *The grey haired and the aged are on our side,*
> *men even older than your father…*
> *listen to me and I will explain to you;*
> *let me tell you what I have seen,*
> *what wise men have declared'*

Job 15:7-18 selected verses

Job is left in no doubt. His friends will not listen to his plea for justice, they will not accept his innocence and they have left him even more isolated than ever. They no longer respect his authority or his wisdom and they pronounce him guilty without a trial. Eliphaz makes this clear by questioning Job's piety, since in his eyes, Job is prepared to charge God with wrong-doing rather than accept fault himself,

> *'you even undermine piety and hinder devotion to*
>   *God.*
> *Your sin prompts your mouth; you adopt the tongue*
>   *of the crafty.*
> *Your own mouth condemns you, not mine;*
> *your own lips testify against you'*   Job 15:4-6

The fate of the wicked

Eliphaz insinuates that in refusing to see reason and repent, Job is making a mockery not only of his own faith but also of belief in God itself. By questioning God's justice he is giving reason for others to doubt God's goodness. Eliphaz is loading Job with the guilt of leading others astray, by his continual rants against God. He believes it is wrong to question what is happening and views Job's continual protestations as letting his emotions get the better of rational judgement. He is allowing anger to cloud his mind, so that he rages against God, when he should realise that in his suffering God is speaking gently to him, drawing him back from sin.

> *'Are God's consolations not enough for you,*
> *words spoken gently to you?*
> *Why has your heart carried you away,*
> *and why do your eyes flash,*
> *so that you vent your rage against God*
> *and pour out such words from your mouth'*
>
> Job 15:11-13

Job has become like the wicked in that he, *'shakes his fist at God and vaunts himself against the Almighty, defiantly charging against him with a thick, strong shield'* (15:25,26). For this, Eliphaz believes, Job will be brought to judgement, and so he proceeds to outline the fate of the wicked (15:20-35) detailing how his wealth will not endure and all that he has established will come to nothing. Bildad continues the attack against Job, seeing him as one who thinks he has a right to special treatment and that God should deal with him differently to how he has treated 'sinners' in the past. Bildad demands to know why all that has been established and known regarding sin and judgement, must be turned upside down, just so that Job can feel justified (18:4). For Bildad the fate of the wicked is clear; his own deeds will bring about his destruction. His health will deteriorate and his days will be filled with terror – exactly as Job has already testified about himself (3:25,26). Disaster will follow him and he will be torn, kicking and screaming, from this life (18:5-16). Zophar continues with the same theme, pointing out that the joy of the wicked is short lived; they will perish forever and fade away like a dream. All they have worked for will have to be repaid, and although evil seems sweet in their mouths, yet it will be as a poison that will kill them. The craving of the wicked will never end, his money will not save him, his guilt will be exposed and an unquenchable fire will consume him (Job 20).

Job's friends present a terrifying picture of the fate of the wicked. In their concern for their friend they have resorted to scare tactics such as those used in drink-driving and anti-smoking campaigns. This doesn't make their statements any less true, but in so doing they are making the strongest possible case that Job's situation can only get worse with no prospect of restitution if he continues to maintain the delusion that he is without fault and therefore God is wrong to judge him. Put in such stark terms it is easy to see why many people picture God as a tyrant. Many atheists question how anyone can sincerely love a God who threatens his creatures with consignment to hell. Even Christians often wonder at the seemingly huge disparity between the God of the Old Testament and Jesus, who is presented in much more loving terms. So how are these views to be reconciled?

God hates sin but loves the sinner

Firstly, it is important that we understand God in terms of his holiness and purity. God and evil are like oil and water in that they cannot mix; their very natures repel one another. Those who walk in God's ways will have a natural affinity for him, just as those who go against his laws will despise and reject him. Since heaven is a state of being in the presence of God and hell is existence without God, those who refuse his call to be reconciled to him, necessarily bring judgement upon themselves. It is a self imposed exile.

Secondly, despite God's inherent, immutable holiness, he still discriminates between a person and their actions, for whilst God hates the sin, he loves the sinner. This helps to revise our thinking particularly in regard to pigeonholing people as mentioned earlier. It also begins to explain how a holy God who cannot tolerate sin can send his one and only Son as an offering of atonement out of love for a 'sinful' people. Whilst we may have a preoccupation with labelling people as sinners, God is more interested in liberating people from their bondage to sin. Whereas society often sees a label as a final description of a person, God sees it as a starting point for restoration.

Is God constrained by moral law?

Thirdly, Job's friends are locked into an unchanging moral view of the universe and of God's dealings with people, whereas God regards us through the sympathetic lens of grace. By this I mean that his friends presuppose God's universe is one in which good is always rewarded and valued, whilst evil is always judged and punished - ultimately by God himself. In this sense there is direct correspondence between what a person does and what they incur as a result; everything is governed by an inevitable causality. Just as planets orbit the sun according to precise laws of motion under the force of gravity, so mankind is to live according to the laws given by God; any deviation will inevitably lead to pain and suffering for the individual and all who become trapped in his orbit. Many accept this mechanistic worldview without question. God has established his laws and moral principles to live by, summarised by the Ten Commandments, which form the foundation of our law system. All people are called to relate to one another according to this defined moral framework. If a person is caught breaking the law they are punished accordingly by strict rules and guidelines. The Ten Commandments do not simply govern our dealing with each other, but also define the way in which we relate to God. If a person sins against God by breaking one of the commandments then that person can expect to be punished unless they repent. We may not like it but that is the way it is - we cannot escape God's gaze and we cannot put forward any defence. We cannot even plead mitigating circumstances for God is the plaintiff, the prosecutor, the witness, the judge and the jury.

This understanding forms the basis of Job's argument for he sees his suffering as a miscarriage of justice with no opportunity for appeal. He vents his rage against God, for what, in his eyes, is a fatally flawed system. Likewise, many today see God as a bully because he takes away from us that which is most precious – our life. As a parent there is often the temptation when trying to control a child to threaten them with taking away a favourite toy or withdrawing a prized privilege. However, when it comes to carrying out the threat it is always difficult because no matter how badly behaved the child, in their eyes the removal of that particular toy or privilege is always regarded as excessive: The punishment always appears greater than the crime. In our relationship with God the same view often persists for people generally do not regard sinning against God as the greatest possible crime one could ever commit. Breaking the Sabbath, worshipping idols or taking his name in vain are not regarded as serious, by comparison with crimes, such as murder and theft. Consequently, being counted as wicked and deserving of hell is regarded as extreme, if not vengeful. But are we right to question God's justice? Are we in a position to decide which crimes are more serious? Are we even right to insist we live in an exclusively moralistic universe? Is Almighty God totally constrained by moral law? Are we right to think of our relationship with him in purely moral terms?

Law is superseded by grace

The bible teaches that though we are given laws to live by, these are not an end in themselves but a springboard to God's work of grace in our lives. In other words, we live in a theistic universe in which moral law is superseded by grace. It is the grace of God and not moral law that primarily motivates God's relationship with us. We see this in the case of Abraham, for even before the law was given, *'Abraham believed God and it was credited to him as righteousness'* (Genesis 17:5). The apostle Paul affirms in his letter to the Romans that Abraham was not justified by obedience to the law, but by faith in the promise of God, concluding *'the promise comes by faith, so that it may be by grace and may be guaranteed to all Abraham's offspring – not only those who are of the law but also to those who are of the faith of Abraham'* (Romans 4:16). The law as represented by the Ten Commandments is not the means by which we are saved but is our schoolmaster leading us to Christ that we may be justified by faith (Galatians 3:24). Paul makes this clear in Romans 6:15 declaring, *'we are not under law but under grace.'* Our final judge is not the law but the Lord. As a king can overrule any decision in a court of law so the Lord has the authority to act in accordance with sovereign grace to all people as he shall choose.

One implication of this is that God regards and treats each person uniquely. In our family we have household rules that we expect to be followed. We also have children of different ages with very different personalities and priorities in their lives. What works for one child does not work for the other! A strong word spoken to one may be all that is required, whereas to another it may be as water off a duck's back and to another totally devastating. We love them all equally but we relate to them in very different ways; we are not constrained by the laws of the house but by our love for them. In the same way God deals with each of us uniquely by grace.

God exercises grace in our lives

Over the next chapters we will unpack this doctrine further, but one immediate application that directly relates to the assertions of Job's friends is that God does not treat us as our sins deserve and if we are disciplined it is always with a view to our restoration: God's punishment is never an end in itself. In society it is one size fits all and one law governs all, with no latitude for mercy and grace, but God is at liberty to exercise his grace in any and every situation that befalls us as he sees fit. For example, two people may commit the same indiscretion; one may be punished, the other pardoned. We might say it's not fair – God says its grace. Two people may be involved in an accident; one may walk away unscathed and the other require medical support for the rest of their lives. We want an explanation. We want clear well defined rules. But God says it is the working out of his grace and mercy, as he declares to Moses *'I will have mercy on whom I will have mercy, and I will have compassion on whom I have compassion'* Exodus 33:19. We make judgements based on our limited understanding and perspective; God sees and knows all things. As a child struggles to understand how a loving parent could allow them to suffer, arguing it is for their good, so we cannot comprehend the gracious purposes of our heavenly Father. Our God sees the bigger picture and it is to his glory that he treats us all uniquely. As with the bag lady it is better to gratefully accept God's grace when it is bestowed than to curse him for our present predicament.

Jesus gives a similar teaching in his parable of the workers in the vineyard (Matthew 20:1-16). He speaks of the kingdom of heaven as being like a landowner who goes out to hire men to work in his vineyard. Throughout the day he employs more and more workers, hiring some at the very last hour. When it comes to pay the workers at the end of the day, all receive the same amount, a denarius. Those employed at the start of the day complain that they have worked longer and harder than those who worked for only one hour. The landowner replies *'Don't I have the right to do what I want with my own money?'* In the same way, God by his grace chooses to bless us all. Even though, in our eyes, some of us are perceived less deserving, before God we are all alienated from him through sin. Is God therefore being unfair if he chooses to treat us all more mercifully than we deserve?

It may be hard to understand and accept this biblical viewpoint especially when it appears God is punishing those who are innocent and vulnerable. We are happy to accept God's mercy when it is bestowed upon us, especially when undeserved, but angry if God appears to withhold from us that which is deemed necessary for our happiness. In an attempt to make sense of this ambiguity, we often take comfort in saying, 'Que sera sera, whatever will be, will be,' as if there is some dispassionate force at work dictating the outcome of our lives. This may appear to get round some of the questions we might have regarding God's love and justice, but it is not biblical and as we shall soon see it can provide no sufficient explanation for the suffering of innocent people. Only through understanding the biblical concept of grace will we be able to understand why we suffer and become more steadfast in our faith and deepen our love for our heavenly Father.

Where do we stand before God?

Whilst acknowledging the importance of grace in God's dealings with us, we must also take heed of the fate of 'the wicked' as put forward by Job's friends, for those who reject God's grace will be judged by the law. It is surely of the utmost importance that we consider where we stand before God's judgement. Many people put their confidence in their own morality as justification for God's acceptance of them. So many times it's said, 'she didn't go to church but she was a good person and kind to everyone she met.' Now I am not saying that church attendance is enough to gain God's pleasure, but Job is finding that neither is pure goodness sufficient. On what moral basis can anyone argue that God is pleased with him or her? Job's blameless life has shown we can no longer rely on our innate goodness. As Job himself argues against his friends, *'Would it turn out well if he examined you? Could you deceive him as you might deceive men?'* (13:9). Jesus berates those Galileans who felt that they were more righteous than those who had suffered at the hands of Pilate, saying,

> *'Do you think these Galileans were worse sinners*
> *than all the other Galileans because they suffered in*
> *this way? I tell you no! But unless you repent, you*
> *too will all perish. Or those eighteen who died when*
> *the tower in Siloam fell on them – do you think*
> *they were more guilty than all the others living in*
> *Jerusalem? I tell you no! But unless you repent, you*
> *too will all perish'*   Luke 13:2-5

Following this call to repentance, Jesus tells the parable of the unfruitful fig tree that fails to bear fruit even after three years of growth. The immediate response is to cut it down, the judgement of moral law, but the gardener asks for one more year to tend it and fertilise it before passing judgement, which is the outworking of grace. Jesus is speaking of a God who sends blessing to encourage fruitfulness rather than bringing about destruction without warning. Throughout the Old Testament God repeatedly sends his prophets to warn his people of their sin demonstrating his reluctance to exact judgement unless it is absolutely necessary. Indeed, the whole sacrificial system was introduced to forestall God's judgement until the coming of our Lord Jesus, who would take upon himself the sins of the people. As the apostle Paul points out, since we could not establish our own righteousness through obedience to God's laws, God made known to us a righteousness through faith in Jesus, by which we can be justified and spared judgement (Romans 3:23-26).

Based on our own morality and conscience we all stand under the judgement of God, and if God were not abundantly gracious to us we would all experience the despair of the wicked each and every day of our lives. Yet, many spend their lives completely oblivious to his loving kindness. Those who live their lives in total disregard of the Lord are surely being presumptuous in insisting God continue to bestow his grace upon them and expecting God forgiveness when they persist in being disobedient. Job has been crying out for a mediator to plead on his behalf and we know that in his mercy God has given us Jesus Christ. The question each must ask is, 'should I receive God's gift of salvation with thankfulness or will I continue to offend God by casting aside the sacrifice of his Son in favour of my own morality?' Do I want to be judged according to the law or by the grace of God?

CHAPTER 7

A King's Ransom (Job 16:1-17:16; 19:1-29)

Her cry evoked the heartbreak of countless men, women and children throughout the ages. It was the sound of Rachel weeping for her children (Matthew 2:16-18), the screams of innocent victims sent to the gas chambers, massacred in ethnic cleansing, murdered through acts of terrorism. It was the cry of those trapped in human trafficking, oppressed by despotic regimes and exploited by the powerful. Her voice demanded our attention, insisted we rise up in judgement against her persecutors. So pitiful and weak, more a whimper than a shout, and yet it haunted our minds, refusing to accept it's cry was not heard, trusting implicitly that one would come, who grieved at the evil and who would judge and rescue the hurting.

'Where is our hope in suffering?' Over the past few chapters we have seen Job struggling to come to terms with his desperate situation. He is grief-stricken, in constant pain from the sores covering his entire body, and accused by his friends of wrongdoing. But Job is not done, either in terms of his fight to maintain his innocence or in his quest to find answers. In response to his friends withering attack, Job once again pours out his complaint declaring God has '*devastated his entire household* (16:7), *assailed him* (16:9), *turned him over to evil men* (16:11), *crushed him* (16:12), *made him his target* (16:12) *and rushed at him like a warrior* (16:14). He concludes, '*my face is red with weeping, deep shadows ring my eyes,*' (16:16) and yet still his hands have been free of violence and his prayer is pure (16:17). Not only has God attacked him without mercy, but his extended family have deserted him; his closest friends detest him, his servants treat him as a stranger and he has become offensive and loathsome to his wife and brothers (Job 19:13-17).

To everyone he is a pariah, someone to be avoided in case there is any guilt incurred by association. They may not voice their judgment, but like Eliphaz, Bildad and Zophar, they believe God is punishing him because of sin, for there has to be a reason. As we have seen, we live in an ordered world and to make sense of that world we must have a moral framework, which states that if you do right you will be blessed and if you do wrong you will be punished. Job is suffering; therefore he is being punished and so Job must have done wrong. The disciples reach the same conclusion when they ask Jesus, '*who sinned, this man or his parents that he was born blind?*' (John 9:2) And for us, when things go wrong, whether it be an oil spill in the Atlantic or a minor accident at work, the response is always 'Who is to blame?'

No one is good enough…

But for Job, nothing makes sense anymore. Everything he thought he knew about God and his dealings with people has been overturned. Until this point in his life he was willing to accept the axioms of a moral universe, believing his goodness was sufficient, even though he was not perfect, because God had blessed him. His argument, and indeed that of his friends, is that if you sincerely do your best and repent if you do something wrong, God will accept you; the good will be saved. What good means is not defined but it is assumed that what is deemed 'good,' is made evident through God's blessing. Furthermore, it is implicit that those who are blessed on earth will also be blessed in the afterlife, whereas those who are not blessed can have no such assurance. The world appears to hold to this maxim except when it comes to the suffering of the innocent, where we struggle to find answers to an apparent contradiction. This is where we find Job, acknowledged by God to be blameless and yet afflicted. The only explanation that can be offered in a monotheistic universe governed by moral law is that Job's goodness is not sufficient. Indeed, no one can meet the standards required of a pure and holy God (Romans 3:23). Whatever we do, no matter how perfect or free of selfishness, can ever be enough for God to be reconciled to us. We are all born and live under judgement, as 'people of the East,' alienated from God, and God is perfectly just in withdrawing his love from us at any time. If he should do that, removing the hedge of love he has placed around us, then Satan will seize the opportunity to inflict misery and pain.

A witness in heaven

However, Job cannot accept this blanket verdict, despite what his friends may say, for he believes God still cares for him and will do everything possible to deliver him from his present crisis. He has spent his entire life 'walking with God', delighting in him and experiencing his pleasure – that must count for something. All those years spent together cannot be forgotten or ignored in a single moment. Otherwise, what's the point of living a righteous life? As Job sits among the ashes, he speaks out again at the injustice of his situation and prays his suffering may ever be held up as a testimony both to the world and before God, *'O earth, do not cover my blood; may my cry never be laid to rest!'* (16:18). His cry is that of the blood of Abel (Genesis 4:10), an unshakeable belief that despite the silence of the heavens, his plight is observed and his cause will be taken up.

As Job muses he becomes convinced he has a witness in heaven who shares his outrage and that this witness is also the advocate and intercessor he has so desperately cried out for earlier,

> *'Even now my witness is in heaven; my advocate is*
> *   on high.*
> *My intercessor is my friend as my eyes pour out tears*
> *   to God;*
> *on behalf of a man he pleads with God as a man*
> *   pleads for his friend'*   Job 16:18-21

Think on the magnitude of these words for a moment. Job is demonstrating the depth of his faith at this crucial point in his life. The writer to the Hebrews states, *'faith is being sure of what we hope for and certain of what we do not see,* (Hebrews

11:1). As Job wrestles with the seeming contradiction of his suffering and a loving God, he reaches out for one who can save him, and whom he is sure must be present. This person will be his advocate, his witness, testifying to his suffering and the integrity of his character, and his friend, who, unlike his human counterparts, will speak truthfully and loyally on his behalf. It is no longer simply Job's word against that of his accuser – he has someone on his side!

A kinsman redeemer

Job yearns for God's reconciliation, but he acknowledges that no one is totally pure and without sin. Therefore, to be truly restored in his relationship with God he needs someone who can and is willing to pay the price of his redemption. In Israelite society there was a custom that in cases of hardship or injustice, the go'el, or kinsman redeemer, would undertake to provide for a family member. For example, a relation may buy back one who has fallen into slavery (Leviticus 25:48) or redeem a field on behalf of a brother or, as in the case of Boaz, marry Ruth, Mahlon's widow, to preserve his relative's inheritance (Ruth 4:9-11). Job is in desperate need of a go'el, but who can redeem him, for as the psalmist states,

> *'no one can redeem the life of another – or give to*
> *God a ransom for him – the ransom of a life is costly,*
> *no payment is ever enough'* Psalm 49:7,8

Elihu picks up this point when he speaks to Job of the need for a mediator,

> *'if there is an angel on his side, as a mediator…*
> *to tell a man what is right for him, to be gracious*
>   *to him and say,*
> *'Spare him from going down to the pit; I have found*
>   *a ransom for him,' –*
> *then his flesh is renewed like a child's;*
> *he prays to God and finds favour with him,*
> *he sees God's face and shouts for joy;*
> *he is restored by God to his righteous state'*
>   Job 33:23-26

In Exodus 6:6-8, the Lord instructs Moses to tell the Israelites that God will act as a go'el to redeem them from slavery in Egypt. He will be their God and bring them into the Promised Land where they will dwell in his presence forever. The only one who is able to pay the price of Job's redemption is God himself and in the case of the people of Israel, God has shown not only that he is willing, but that he is obligated to do so, for he has adopted them as his own. With this imagery firmly in focus and seeing by faith his witness in heaven, Job prays what must be the most audacious prayer in Holy Scripture,

> *'Give me, O God, the pledge that you demand.*
> *Who else will put up security for me?'*   Job 17:3

Imagine a man standing in the dock after being pronounced guilty of a crime by the jury. The judge calls for everyone to stand as he passes sentence. He takes a black hat and places it upon his head and announces that the punishment is the death penalty. There's a gasp from the courtroom as all eyes fix upon the man standing in the dock. The judge turns to the man and asks if he has any last words to say before he is taken away. The man, head bowed in shame, glances up and gazes deep into the judge's eyes, 'will you pay the price for me? Will you take my place?'

An audacious request

How can Job possibly ask God to take his place? Surely it is presuming too much of their relationship? Why should God lay down his life for a creature his hands have made? Why should God sacrifice himself for one who is so lowly and inconsequential? Yet Job feels emboldened to ask, despite all that has happened, for he remains convinced God loves him and longs to be in communion with him – whatever the cost, whatever the crime! Indeed, his past relationship with God is such that he believes God is obligated to help him, for Job is his servant. Job sees in this selfless act by God, not only his vindication but also the strengthening of all those who have put their faith in God (Isaiah 38:18,19). Eliphaz has argued that Job's refusal to accept his sin will ultimately create a spirit of rebellion among believers for they will question God's justice and doubt his goodness (15:4). But Job is convinced he is wrong; although God has brought Job to his knees, yet *the righteous will hold to their ways, and those with clean hands will grow stronger'* (17:9), for they will see the mercy and grace of God in his deliverance of Job. Indeed, the righteous will praise God all the more for they will see that he is able to rescue his people to the uttermost. In the midst of his suffering, Job is finding hope, for he sees the Almighty God as the lover of his soul, who will answer his prayer and personally undertake his redemption.

Finding hope

As Job reflects on God putting up his security, he rejects his initial request that he be allowed to die (3:11-19), finally recognising that if all he has to look forward to is the grave, then there is no hope in life at all (17:13-16); life without God is a mockery, having no meaning and no absolute purpose, but God created mankind to be in relationship with the divine being. As Augustine has said, *'he has put eternity into the heart of man.'* As Job considers the loving kindness of God, his need for, and God's provision of, a redeemer comes into full view and he gives voice to the certainty of a renewed hope,

> *'I know that my redeemer lives,*
> *and that in the end he will stand upon the earth.*
> *And after my skin has been destroyed,*
> *yet in my flesh I will see God;*
> *I myself will see him with my own eyes –*
> *I, and not another. How my heart yearns within me!'*
>
> Job 19:25-27

Job is convinced God has provided a redeemer, who will bring him back into the presence of God. Furthermore, although this redeemer is in heaven, he firmly believes that one day he will stand upon the earth, that all may behold him. Yet what most captivates Job's imagination and fills him with an overwhelming sense of joy and yearning is his firm belief that one day he will meet his Saviour, face to face.

Jesus our redeemer

Job's faith in God's provision of a redeemer is not unfounded. There is indeed a redeemer, appointed by God, who undertakes to save all who turn to him - the Lord Jesus Christ. Jesus is our intercessor, our witness and our friend; he is our advocate, our ransom and our hope. In a court of law a reliable witness can make all the difference in ensuring justice is delivered. In Jesus we have one who is recognised by God as exemplary, whose testimony can be relied on unequivocally and whose credentials are without equal. Indeed, it is for this reason that God our Father, has called upon him to represent us. Moreover, our witness is the King of kings and Lord of lords! What an honour to have the King, acting on our behalf, for who could dare challenge his testimony. Furthermore, he is the Judge's one and only Son, whose influence must necessarily be great, for not only does he have the full respect of his Father but he also knows exactly how to present our case, so as to convince him to uphold our cause and to bring about our deliverance. In all your suffering, may you know that even now Jesus is your witness in the courts of heaven, presenting your case with all his divine authority, influence and wisdom. God has appointed him specifically to represent you and he will do his uttermost to ensure you receive justice and salvation. If you are alone, if you feel that you have no voice and that no-one hears your cries, then be assured that the King of kings is even now speaking on your behalf before the throne of God; though the world may forsake you, the Lord Jesus will never give you up and no-one can snatch you from the hollow of his hand (John 10:10).

Not only is Jesus an incomparable witness, but he is also your most loyal friend. He has left the courts of heaven to rescue you, he has clothed himself with poverty and shame that he might raise you up and crown you with honour – because he loves you, he has laid down his very life for you (John 15:13). Have you ever asked yourself, what you have ever done for him, that he should devote himself to your welfare and deliverance? Have you denied him through fear of what others might say? He will never deny you! Have you failed him in service? He will not fail you! Have you grieved his Spirit by the way you have lived? He will never cause you to question his loyalty. Though all betray you, he will not suffer even a hair on your head to be harmed (Luke 21:16-19). There is nothing you can do to deserve his love and compassion – and there is nothing you can do to make him withdraw his love and compassion from you. Even now the Lord Jesus extends his hand to you, will you take it? You may feel like Peter, so overwhelmed that you see yourself sinking beneath the waves, but your Saviour and friend, whispers in the midst of the storm *'Take courage! It is I, Don't be afraid'* (Matthew 14:27). You may, on hearing his still small voice, cry out in desperation, 'Lord, save me!' Immediately, he will reach out to catch you, saying, *'You of little faith, why did you doubt?'* (Matthew 14:22-31). As the hymn writer proclaims, 'what a friend we have in Jesus, all our sins and grief to bear; what a privilege to carry everything to God in prayer.'

God loves you

I spoke earlier of Job's audacious prayer, *'Give me O God, the pledge you demand. Who else will put up security for me?'* (17:3). In Jesus, God has given Job his reply, and it is yes! I will pay the price for your redemption. So many people speak of a God who is distant, of a God who does not care, who does not understand the human condition, who is hard and unyielding. Yet, here we have Almighty God answering the prayer of a man who is suffering and plagued with doubt; a God who says that he has appointed a witness to testify on our behalf and a redeemer who will take our place, shoulder all our burdens and bear all our sin that we might be restored to him. Here we have a God who says, 'I love you so much, I am ready and willing to die for you.' Here we have a God who says, when I promise to be your Father and make you my child, I undertake to do all that is necessary to rescue you and restore you to myself. I will not abandon you or leave you helpless (Hebrews 13:5,6).

These are not the words of a tyrant who is insensitive to the needs of his people. These are not the actions of a God who is constrained by moral law, but the voice of a sovereign God who treats us according to his mercy and grace. In the place of judgement, in his darkest hour, our kinsman redeemer, the Lord Jesus, offers up his life blood and declares to the world 'it is finished.' In Christ a new covenant has been established, not based on obedience to the law but through grace, obtained by faith in Jesus our ransom. As the writer to the Hebrews says,

> *'Christ is the mediator of a new covenant, that those who are called may receive the promised eternal inheritance – now that he has died as a ransom to set them free from the sins committed under the first covenant'* Hebrews 9:15

As yet, we may not see an immediate end to our suffering or our feelings of abandonment, *'but we see Jesus, crowned with glory and honour because he suffered death, so that by the grace of God he might taste death for everyone'* (Hebrews 2:9). We see our inheritance in heaven and the final redemption of our bodies. By faith in Christ, you can know for certain that God has created you for glory, for the praise of his name, and when you, as member of the church of Christ, stand before him on the last day, all the heavenly host will worship him, because he has redeemed you and brought you forth as gold to be his most precious bride.

The darkness and cold of winter can seem so long, yet with the coming of spring, the sun's rays awaken the earth and under gentle April showers, shoots push through the softened earth; animals stir from their slumber and venture out from their gloomy dungeons to discover a new world waiting for them. So, too, the day of our redemption draws near, when we will arise, to receive our glorious inheritance and be with our Lord forever, bathed in the radiance of his glory. Therefore, let us strengthen our feeble knees and faltering hearts and in this hope let us declare with Paul

> *'I consider that our present sufferings are not worth comparing with the glory that will be revealed in us… the redemption of our bodies.*
> *For in this hope we were saved. But hope that is seen is no hope at all.*
> *Who hopes for what he already has?*
> *But if we hope for what we do not yet have, we wait for it patiently'* Romans 8:18-25

We began asking the question, 'Where is our hope in suffering?' The answer is Jesus. He is our hope, our glory and our crown.

CHAPTER 8

Suffering and Grace (Job 21:1-34)

Frank was a thorn in his side. He was popular, fit, handsome and wealthy, everything Graham wanted to be. He gambled and won – often, he was sickening lucky. He had a gorgeous wife and was never ever ill, not even a toothache. He had the perfect job and an even better retirement package. In short he had everything, but that wasn't the real aggravation for Graham. Like a constantly dripping tap or a nagging woman, he delighted in mocking Graham's faith day after day. Graham tried to avoid him but he was persistent, determined to rescue his erring neighbour by proving God didn't exist. Night after weary night Graham prayed for God to intervene – nothing happened. Instead it was Graham who became desperately ill and the doctor called Frank to watch over him!

We concluded last time with the wondrous revelation given to Job of a witness in heaven and a kinsman redeemer who is none other than the Lord Jesus Christ. We have seen that if we have put our faith in him, we have a steadfast hope, even in the midst of our suffering, that God loves us, has saved us and has an inheritance stored up for us in heaven. Like Job, we can know that one day we will see our Saviour face to face, and on that day we will bow down in worship before him, with tears in our eyes and praise on our lips. This is indeed a blessed assurance but it still hasn't brought us to the point where we can fully understand our suffering. For if, through faith in Jesus, we have been redeemed and enjoy favour with God, then why do we continue to suffer while those who break God's law and reject his call seem to live a carefree life?

What of the ungodly?

This point is brought to the fore in Job's final response to Zophar in chapter 21, where he repudiates the claim that the wicked spend their life in misery. Far from it he insists, they have all they want:

> 'Why do the wicked live on, growing old and
>   increasing in power?
> They see their children established around them,
> their offspring before their eyes.
> Their homes are safe and free from fear;
> the rod of God is not upon them'   Job 21:7-9

He goes on to argue that their flocks and herds flourish as do their children, and their lives are filled with music and merriment,

> *'they spend their days in prosperity*
> *and go down to the grave in peace.*
> *Yet, they say to God, 'Leave us alone!*
> *We have no desire to know your ways.*
> *Who is the Almighty, that we should serve him?*
> *What would we gain by praying to him?...*
> *yet how often does calamity come upon them,*
> *the fate that God allots in his anger?'*

Job 21:13-17

We can sympathise with Job, for we hear the same argument today and we ourselves may have reached the same conclusion. Why is it that a sincere Christian may be plagued with ill health, be consistently knocked back at work and discriminated against because of his faith, while his atheist colleague, who is forever humiliating him because of his beliefs, never seems to have any problems, always falls on his feet and does whatever he wishes? Again, it is not unusual for new believers to go through a period of intense suffering after coming to faith in God. Many could say, 'my life was OK until I became a Christian. It's then that all the trouble started! You'd think that God would bless me not punish me!' In the midst of these incongruities it's not surprising many believers question their faith, make compromises in their walk with God and envy the lives of those who are openly hostile towards God.

For Job, the accepted wisdom of his day that insisted *'God stores up a man's punishment for his sons,'* (21:19), cut no ice, for he could see no advantage in this as a means of restraining sin. It lacked the power to control the ungodly, for *'what do the wicked care about the suffering of those who come after them?'* (Job 21:21, Isaiah 39:5-8). Instead, he argues that those who sin should see their own destruction and experience the consequences of their own actions. We can surely empathise with Job. Humanity lives for the moment and finds delayed judgement a very difficult concept to live by; punishment needs to be clearly linked to wrongful behaviour. A child cannot be punished two days after an offence was committed! Advertising campaigns pointing out the dangers of smoking or driving whilst under the influence of alcohol or drugs meet with limited success unless accompanied by on the spot fines, imprisonment or increased tax duty. This is not limited to individuals, as the global warming agenda clearly demonstrates, with nations reluctant to significantly reduce their carbon footprint in the light of more immediate political concerns. The call that we are bequeathing a polluted world to our children apparently makes little impression on policy.

But no one can teach God wisdom, admits Job; it matters not whether a man is godly or whether he does evil. One man may live a rich life, enjoying health, wealth and security. Another may be cursed with poverty and despair, yet both will surely share the same fate, (21:23-26); there is no earthly reward for the righteous. To Job, it seems unjust that an evil person should be spared 'the day of calamity' and that no one should *'repay him for what he has done'* (21:29-31). How is anyone to recognise God's love for his people if the innocent are seen to suffer whereas those who carry out evil prosper, even though they spurn God himself? What comfort is it to have an advocate in heaven, interceding on behalf of the righteous, if such a mediator is seemingly not needed in the case of the ungodly, since God withholds his judgement of them?

Suffering awakens us to our need

In order to begin to offer an explanation we need to once again challenge the accepted wisdom that states we live in a world in which the things that happen to us are dictated by the moral choices we make, in the same way a particular cause will always have a specific predetermined effect. We must question the axiom that those who do that which is morally good are always rewarded and those who choose to do evil are punished accordingly. The problem with this view is that the good are not always blessed and the bad are not always punished, as Job has pointed out already. If we were applying rigorous scientific method to this hypothesis we would throw it out immediately because it does not fit observation. However, we are stubborn people who refuse even to re-examine our conviction for not only does it provide a moral explanation of the universe that appeals to our conscience, but it also instils the belief that we can determine the outcome of our lives. Arguably the biggest selling point of the Labour manifesto under Tony Blair was 'Education, education, education,' with the tantalising carrot that if we only knew more we could make the right moral choices and create our own utopia. Despite the obvious point that even the most educated people still commit crimes, we continue to hold on to the certainty that the good are blessed and the bad are punished, whilst turning a blind eye to the ambiguity of innocent suffering, choosing to blame God for anything that doesn't seem to fit our model.

C.S. Lewis has argued that 'suffering is God's megaphone to a deaf world.'[1] He contends that suffering awakens us to our need of God, pointing out that it is seldom when we are content that we seek after God; but when in the midst of trouble, all manner of individuals, believers and non-believers alike are observed to pray. Taking this one step further it can be suggested that God permits the innocent to suffer and the wicked to thrive to make us realise that we are building our lives on a faulty premise. Day after day God reveals to us that it is by grace we are saved and not by works, by allowing the morally bad to flourish and the innocent to suffer. He turns all our thinking upside down – and yet we continue to blind ourselves to his truth. No one is good enough to get to heaven without God's grace, not the morally bad nor the morally good. We all stand under condemnation; we are all alienated from God. As we have seen in the previous chapters, we all need a mediator to intercede for us. We all need a redeemer who will pay the price for our sin, for as Paul makes clear, *'there is no difference, for all have sinned and fall short of the glory of God, and are justified freely by his grace through the redemption that came by Christ Jesus'* (Romans 3:23,24).

We could argue and many do, that this is inconsistent with the notion of a loving God. How can a God of love continue to allow the innocent to suffer, often at the hands of evil people, in order to convince us that we do not live in an inflexible moral universe? There are a number of possible responses to this, each of which takes us deeper into our understanding of God and of the human condition.

We cannot buy God's love

Firstly, God would have us understand that we cannot buy his love. Children can sometimes become caught in the middle of a nasty divorce settlement in which a parent tries to win their affection, perhaps by procuring expensive gifts or taking them on exciting holidays. In such cases the other parent may argue, 'you cannot buy a child's love,' implying that what the child most needs is relationship. Alternatively, a child may present 'an apple' to his teacher in an attempt to win her favour. God does not want us to believe we can effectively buy our way into his affection, through doing good deeds, for it creates a wrong basis for the relationship he desires. He delights in us when we do good things and he is sad when we wilfully break his laws, but our behaviour does not affect his love for us, which is the love of a father for his child (Deuteronomy 7:7-9).

Living within a moral framework we make the mistake of thinking we need to, and in fact are able to, earn his love. God, because he is truth and love, would not have us deceived, spending our lives striving after something that does not gain us access to his presence. For this reason the apostle Paul gives his sternest criticism to the Church in Galatia (Galatians 3:1-14). Consider how you would feel on arriving at the gates of heaven after living an abstemious and austere life only to be told it wasn't necessary and in any case you hadn't done enough! God wants us to know from the outset that it is through putting our faith in Christ and in his righteousness that we are counted worthy and received into heaven – not on the basis of what we have done. By permitting all people, and especially the godly to suffer, he is declaring to all people that good works are insufficient to merit salvation.

We are perhaps justifiably angry that God should allow the innocent and vulnerable to suffer, yet we do not realise the consequences if God should allow us to carry on in our deception concerning our moral eligibility. By continuing to put our trust in our own merit, we will be excluded from his presence, his love and his gracious involvement in our lives for all eternity – and that would indeed be hell: Jesus describes such a state as a place *'of weeping and gnashing of teeth'* (Matthew 22:13). This would be far worse than anything we presently suffer in this world, no matter how great our pain and our grief may appear. I do not say this lightly, for every day we hear stories of innocent people who suffer under the most appalling circumstances and conditions, in some cases worse than our most horrific nightmares. But, we need to remember that to keep us from 'hell' Jesus endured the greatest suffering ever borne by any human being. In the Garden of Gethsemane, he was so overwhelmed and distressed by what he had to face, that his sweat fell to the ground like drops of blood (Luke 22:44) and he prayed earnestly that, if it were possible, God would spare him this suffering. It was because God loves you and I that he stood by and watched his one and only Son, mocked, whipped, beaten and crucified on a cross. He did nothing to stop his suffering, though it must have broken his heart, because he wanted to save you and I, through Christ paying the price for our ransom. Our heavenly Father sent his Son into the world, and Jesus went in obedience to the cross to spare us all, from even greater suffering than we or anyone else are presently experiencing.

Suffering takes us more deeply into God's love

God is able to use suffering to take his children more deeply and fully into his love. For those, like Job, who truly love him, will seek after him and cry out to him in their distress all the more urgently and fervently and find in him the source of all their joy and hope. As a hurting child will run past all other family and friends and throw herself into the arms of her mother, so the godly will turn away from all other sources of potential comfort to cast themselves into the loving arms of

God – and in that coming together, such will be the experience of comfort, joy and security that all hurt will fade away to be replaced with a deep and lasting peace and assurance. I have observed that those with the greatest love for the Lord and the deepest assurance of his peace are those who have faced the greatest storms in life and most often walked through the valley of the shadow of death. It is in those experiences they have found the strength, comfort and deliverance of their heavenly Father. In contrast, those who have never known the Lord have no such assurance and in times of trouble find no rock to cling to or love to hold them fast.

Not everyone can be good

Secondly, God allows the righteous to suffer because not everyone can be good. We live in a world where our circumstances are not always under our personal control. The experiences we face can seriously affect the way we behave and relate to others. Children brought up by abusive parents, victims of bullying or rape, those taken for sexual exploitation, or who become addicted to drugs cannot always do 'the right thing,' as required by law. Those who are nurtured in more positive environments can therefore be said to have an unfair advantage if moral lifestyle were the prime factor for access to heaven. Not everyone can be good, but everyone can believe. From the youngest to the oldest, the best to the worst, the weakest to the strongest, all have the opportunity to receive the gift of life that is freely offered in Jesus Christ (Galatians 3:26-28). Knowing that we can break free of our past life is a most glorious truth of the gospel. It gives us hope to persevere and it sustains us in times of darkness, for it is an eternal light at the end of a very dark tunnel. Allowing the 'righteous' to suffer points to the need for some other means of salvation, which can be for all and which is not exclusive to those who have the right upbringing or who are born with the right postcode!

We cannot change our past

Related to this is that however much we might want it, we cannot undo our past. Once a sin has been committed it can never be undone and neither can the guilt associated with it ever be washed away. As Lady Macbeth cries out following the murder of Duncan, *'Will all great Neptune's ocean wash this blood clean from my hand?'* [2] In a moral universe the rules are clear – one strike and you're out. We live forever with the consequences of our sin with no hope of reprieve (Genesis 3:17-24), for once a 'sinner' always a 'sinner'. Job's insistence on his integrity was all the hope he could cling to until his redeemer was revealed to him. In Christ we have one who came to seek and to save the lost. Jesus lived a perfect, spotless life and by putting our faith in him we are clothed in his righteousness, and therefore declared holy before God for all eternity.

In this way, Jesus is both our hope and our motivation for growing in holiness. At first sight we might think this would take away all motivation, since our actions do not count against us providing we put our faith in Christ. But being clothed in Christ's righteousness enables us to seek more confidently and earnestly after holiness. For example, consider two women diagnosed with a debilitating illness, one of whom receives ground-breaking medication that will ensure her full recovery. Knowing this, she will be able to endure her daily struggles more courageously and live an arguably more full life than the other who suffers with no hope of a cure. In the same way, knowing we have been cleansed from sin and counted righteous through faith, we are set free to strive to live a godly life, seeking to attain that degree of life and holiness which we have already been granted (Philippians 3:12-14). Furthermore, we have the additional encouragement that no matter how many times we may fall short of what is required, we have the gospel promise that, *'if we confess our sins, he is faithful and just and will forgive us our sins and cleanse us from all unrighteousness'* (1 John 1:9).

We are not being punished

Thirdly, God would have us know that our suffering is not punishment for sin. The common consensus is that people suffer as a punishment for the things they have done. However, God would have us know that all our sin and guilt has been placed upon Christ. For Christ *'himself bore our sins in his body on the tree, so that we might die to sins and live for righteousness; by his wounds you have been healed'* (1 Peter 2:24). Consequently, whatever suffering we may experience, it is not God's punishment for sin, for if in Christ we confess and seek forgiveness our sin and guilt are expunged. We are reminded of this every time we confess and receive the 'Absolution'. Knowing we are not being chastised by a vengeful God is something we need to keep close to our hearts for one of Satan's greatest weapons is to deceive us into thinking God desires our destruction.

God does not punish us, but he does use suffering to purify us - not to save us, but to sanctify us for the glory of God. An adopted child is welcomed as a fully-fledged member of the family, but he still needs to be disciplined in how he is to live within his newfound family. He needs to be weaned off some of his old ways and taught new principles and priorities. A child who is not a member of the family receives no such instruction (Hebrews 12:5-12). If you are suffering as a Christian, take heart for God is treating you as his beloved son or daughter, perfecting in you the work of Christ. Again, as a skilled craftsman chisels away at a rough piece of marble to create a work of art that reflects his character, so God is at work in each of us, sculpting, shaping and polishing us until we reflect the glory of Christ.

We are not to fear the future

Finally, God allows the good to suffer because he doesn't want us to live in fear of the future. Many sincere Christians become very anxious as they approach the end of their days, in case they have not fully met the requirements of God's law. They have no assurance their lives are holy and good enough[3]. John Wesley on his conversion writes,

> 'my whole heart is 'altogether corrupt and
>   abominable'…
> that 'alienated' as I am from the life of God,
> I am 'a child of wrath', and heir of hell:..
> that, 'having the sentence of death' in my heart,
> and having nothing in or of myself to plead,
> I have no hope but that of being justified freely
> 'through the redemption that is in Jesus'[4]

God does not want us to live as though we had the sword of Damocles hanging over us. He wants us to enjoy all the benefits of the life he has given us. To enable this he must break down any association we have between acceptance and morality, for only then will we experience true joy and freedom. God loves you because you are his child, through faith in Jesus, not because of anything you have done or haven't done. We cannot earn his love, we do not deserve his love, but we can and must receive his love. In view of all this, it is essential that we abandon all emphasis on good works as a means to acceptance with God and instead put all our faith and hope in the person and work of Jesus Christ. He alone has lived a perfect life, without spot or taint of sin. He alone is worthy to pay the ransom for our souls (Revelation 4:9)!

1. Lewis, C. S. (1940) The Problem of Pain: Harper Collins Publishers, London
2. Shakespeare, W. (1983) Macbeth: Illustrated Stratford Shakespeare, Chancellor Press Act 2 Scene 2
3. Dallimore, A (1995) George Whitfield. Banner of Truth Trust. Vol. 2 pg. 262
4. Dallimore, A (1995) George Whitfield. Banner of Truth Trust. Vol. 1 pg. 179,180

CHAPTER 9

Suffering and Judgement (Job 22:1-27:23)

Susie waited at the prison gates with some trepidation. She was due to meet the man who killed her daughter, whilst driving under the influence of drugs. It was part of a restorative justice programme but she wasn't sure she could go through with it. A warder ushered her in and sat her opposite the one who'd destroyed her life. For a long time she said nothing, just stared at the floor. Eventually, she forced herself to ask generally about his life in prison. His cell was reasonable, food not bad and there were numerous courses and opportunities to better oneself. He spoke confidently, assured and Susie found herself unfavourably comparing his life with her own now her daughter was dead. 'Was this justice, was he sorry?' She began to speak of her pain, the emptiness of her days, the long nights she had lain awake crying. She stopped, suddenly aware he was sobbing. He rose from the chair, came over and fell at her feet, begging for her forgiveness.

We considered in the last chapter the possibility God may permit the innocent to suffer and the wicked prosper, to teach us that salvation is by grace through faith and not by good works (Ephesians 2:9,10). It may be that this still leaves many questions unanswered and issues unresolved, not least concerning the apparent freedom of those who abuse their power and cause misery to the lives of others. It may be that you are experiencing something like that even now and are confused and angry with God for not protecting you from harm. Like Job, you may be questioning why God should be so interested in probing every part of your life, searching out the slightest blunders and blemishes (10:6,20), while seemingly turning a blind eye to the barefaced brutality of your tormentors.

For Eliphaz, such questions are an attack on the holiness of God's justice, which he is zealous to uphold. In his hearing, Job has criticised God's justice by suggesting 'the wicked' live untroubled, prosperous lives, whilst boldly declaring, *'who is the Almighty that we should serve him? What would we gain by praying to him?'* (21:15). Such censure is too much for Eliphaz, who interprets these statements as putting man above God. Far from debating the value of serving God, Job should be considering what benefit to God is man's righteousness,

> *'Can a man be of benefit to God? Can even a wise*
> *   man benefit him?*
> *What pleasure would it give the Almighty if you*
> *   were righteous?*
> *What would he gain if your ways were blameless?*

> *Is it for your piety that he rebukes you and brings*
> *charges against you?*
> *Is not your wickedness great and are not your sins*
> *endless?'* Job 22:2-5

Eliphaz is surely right to assert that we are the created and God is the Creator. As such God is complete within himself and requires nothing from his creation in any way, shape or form. He receives no benefit from even our most righteous deeds and is under no obligation to bestow any blessing upon anything that he has made. For this reason, we should not expect God to reward us, even if we wholeheartedly fulfil his will, as our Lord says to his disciples, *'so you also, when you have done everything you were told to do, should say, 'We are unworthy servants; we have only done our duty'* (Luke 17:10).

Eliphaz' slanderous accusations

However, Eliphaz is frustrated by Job's insistence that God should grant him an audience as if the created could order about the Creator. Such arrogance stirs him to attack Job's alleged piety, firstly by challenging his righteousness and secondly by asserting very forcefully, that Job's suffering is a direct result of his great wickedness. Eliphaz slanders Job's name, falsely accusing him of breaking God's laws and stressing that Job committed all of his 'crimes' even though he was wealthy and held in great honour,

> *'You demanded security from your brothers for no*
> *reason;*
> *you stripped men of their clothing, leaving them naked.*

> *You gave no water to the weary and you withheld*
>   *food from the hungry,*
> *though you were a powerful man,*
> *owning land – an honoured man, living on it.*
> *And you sent widows away empty handed*
> *and broke the strength of the fatherless.*
> *That is why snares are all around you, why sudden*
>   *peril terrifies you,*
> *why it is so dark that you cannot see,*
> *and why a flood of water covers you'*   Job 22:6-11

In attempting to uphold God's justice and maintain his moral worldview, Eliphaz has concocted unsubstantiated allegations against Job and vilified his friend. Job has insisted he stands aloof from the council of the wicked (21:16), but Eliphaz throws his protestations back in his face (22:12-18), declaring he has behaved wickedly and is clearly being judged: However Job might seek to cover up his offences, God is just and sees all. Yet, if he repents, God will hear his prayers and answer him, saving the downcast and delivering, even those who are not innocent, through the cleanness of Job's hands (22:23-30). One might ask why, if this is true, Eliphaz does not pray for Job that he might be delivered from his suffering!

Job just wants to meet with God

Whilst we may respect Eliphaz' zealousness for God, his words are not based on knowledge (Romans 10:2), but on a desire to establish his own righteousness. Although Job accepts that man cannot benefit God in any way, his relationship with the Almighty is altogether different to that of Eliphaz. He knows God as a faithful friend, who loves him and who in the past has bestowed great blessing upon him. His understanding of the master servant relationship is more akin to that given by Jesus in his parable of the master finding his servants waiting for him, *'he will dress himself to serve, will have them recline at the table and will come and wait on them,'* (Luke 12:35-37). God is under no obligation to bestow blessings on his people, but he is a God of love, and cannot help but delight in giving good things. This continues to be the source of Job's confusion (23:1). He cannot reconcile his sense of abandonment with a God who is prepared to pay the price of his redemption.

Job longs to come before God, so that he can voice his complaint, for he is convinced that he will be completely exonerated (23:7). For the whole of his life, he has walked blamelessly in obedience to God's commands and treasured God's words even more than food (23:11,12), but now he doesn't know where to find God! No matter how much he cries out for help, the heavens are as brass. It may be that this is a picture of how you are feeling at the moment; whereas once you walked with God in close and tender fellowship, as the closest of friends, you feel now that God is a stranger. Like the psalmist you want to cry out,

> *'How long O Lord? Will you forget me for ever?*
> *How long will you hide your face from me?*
> *How long must I wrestle with my thoughts*
> *and every day have sorrow in my heart?*
> *How long will my enemy triumph over me?*
>
> Psalm 13:1,2

A time for judgement

Job feels trapped in a situation that is not of his making. He dreads what more may happen to him, plans that God still has in store and yet he refuses to give way to fear for that is to abandon hope entirely. He cannot understand why God does not set a time for judgement so that the wicked may be punished and the innocent set free? It seems to him that those who oppress the vulnerable are left alone, whilst the poor and those who have no one to represent them go about naked, hungry and cold (24:2-12). Furthermore, those who rebel against the light in order to murder, steal and commit adultery appear to do so with impunity (24:13-17). To Job it appears as if God has a soft spot for the wicked whilst being harsh and uncompromising to his own.

As Job wrestles with this dilemma, he considers the ultimate destiny of 'the wicked,' recognising that those who do evil have no lasting benefit or presence in the world: They are as foam on the water, or melting snow (24:18,19). Though they may be raised up for a time and feel secure, they have no lasting assurance of life and will be brought low like everyone else (24:18-24). In such circumstances Job would rather have his integrity for at least he could stand before God's judgement seat with a clear conscience (27:1-6). Indeed, he argues, what hope have the godless when God takes away their life? *'Does God listen to his cry when distress comes upon him? Will he find delight in the almighty? Will he call upon God at all times?'* (Job 27:9,10). He makes the point that those who disown God will not call upon him and neither can they expect an answer in time of need. Their fate is destruction and their destiny the grave. All he has established will be taken from him and given to the righteous. The one who does evil builds on sand; his house is like a moth's cocoon, easily crushed; a temporary residence, like a watchman's hut. When he lies down in death all will be gone and he will have nothing. Terror will seize him and he will be carried off by the east wind - driven forever from God's presence (Job 27:21-22). Job concludes that although 'the wicked' may become established in this life and able to sin with impunity, when it comes to their final destiny they will go to the grave and be cut off from God forever. Although 'the righteous' will also die he believes they still have the prospect of being united with God.

Different responses to suffering

We may understand Job's reasoning by contrasting the response of the righteous and the ungodly to suffering. The righteous, epitomised by Job, desire to dwell in God's presence all their days. They are not content simply with blessings being bestowed upon them, no matter how great they may be, for they yearn most for God himself, without whom all blessings are meaningless. When suffering comes and God seems to be absent, they cry out and plead for him, as a child will cry for a parent. When that parent responds and takes the child into his or her arms, the child is comforted because it once again knows the security and love of the parent. In the same way, the believer finds peace and security in his/her renewed relationship with God and faith is made stronger.

The ungodly, however, take whatever blessing comes their way without thought to the giver, for they do not know God. When suffering comes, they mourn and express anger at what is happening, yet they do not seek after God but rather blame him. So it is that suffering brings the godly closer to God but drives the ungodly further away. As Job has already intimated the righteous cry out to their advocate that he may pray on their behalf and bring their needs to God, but the unbeliever has no such assurance of faith. In death, the righteous cry out to God and are heard because of their reverent submission, but the wicked have their alienation confirmed and are carried away to an eternity without God. In this way Job begins to see that suffering is a touchstone for recognising those who have a true love for God and those who refuse to live under the shadow of his wings.

This explanation may help us to appreciate the manner in which God dispenses justice. Job queries why has God not set times for judgement so that the world may see and take note that he is active in his world, punishing sin and overturning injustice. Yet, if we consider the manner in which loving parents discipline their children, we will quickly see a difference between an obedient and wilful child. Disciplining an obedient child will instruct them and help them to grow in godliness, but punishing an unruly child will only serve to harden their heart (Proverbs 15:5). Likewise, those who respond to the discipline of suffering, grow in godliness, whereas those who reject discipline become increasingly defiant. This is not to say that God does not judge the ungodly, but that he recognises that even though they have the law, they have rejected it as having any authority over their lives. Punishment will not make such people accept the law, but hate it all the more, for shaming them and alienating them from society and God. It may be objected that in this view the law is seen to be powerless and provides little incentive for moral behaviour. This is true and indeed we see the evidence for this in our legal system and prisons today: The law has scant capacity to change behaviour. Paul makes a similar point in his letter to the Romans where he cries out that his sinful nature opposes the law of God (Romans 7:14-20). Consequently, the law is powerless to make us godly because it is weakened by our sinful nature (Romans 8:3), which is why our only hope is in Christ Jesus.

Righteous suffering draws the ungodly to God

If we accept the premise that exacting punishment on those who are rebellious towards God generally only serves to increase their defiance, the question naturally arises as to how can a God of love, who is unwilling that any should perish, draw the ungodly to himself. Paradoxically, the answer may be through the suffering of the righteous.

Firstly, whilst an immoral person may become even more rebellious if punished for his crimes, he may seek amendment when he witnesses those he regards as more principled being punished for lesser indiscretions. For example, a newly qualified teacher was given a difficult class to teach. Her head of year informed her of the more undisciplined children and those from whom she should expect little trouble. On entering the classroom, she observed one of the latter speaking quietly to a classmate while she was introducing herself. For this she awarded a strict punishment. The other pupils, observing the teacher was not one to be trifled with behaved impeccably throughout the lesson. In similar manner the suffering of the righteous can be more of a deterrent to those who rebel against authority than their own punishment, for it allows them to consider the consequences of their actions in the light of what is happening to others. It also raises the prospect that if those who are good and enjoy favour with God suffer in this way, then what will happen to those who are openly disobedient. If God disciplines those he loves, what awaits those who are under his wrath (1 Peter 4:17-18)!

Righteous suffering brings people to faith

Secondly, the suffering of the innocent can serve to call people to faith, for when unbelievers witness righteous people clinging to their faith and praising God in the midst of great hardship and trial it directs them to a deeper reality. Even atheists, who are wholly opposed to the very notion of God, will listen and respect the faith of one who believes and can sincerely worship God in the midst of unjust suffering. For when they observe such faith in action, it opens their eyes to the fact that they are spiritual orphans, without a loving heavenly Father to guide and instruct them. It highlights to them that in a similar position they would have no hope, no rock to cling to, no saviour to call upon and no arms of love in which to find security and peace. Such was the experience of the Philippian jailor, who on seeing Paul and Silas in their cells praising God, cried out, *'Sirs, what must I do to be saved?'* (Acts 16:30). It is with this in mind that the apostle Peter calls those who suffer unjustly, not to be afraid but always to be *'prepared to give an answer to everyone who asks you to give a reason for the hope that you have,'* (1 Peter 3:15), for godly suffering hones faith and helps a Christian to speak with greater depth and authority concerning belief in God and the joy of living in a loving relationship with the Lord.

Righteous suffering changes priorities

Thirdly, suffering can help those who desire to live godly lives become less superficial both in their relationships and in their outlook on life, particularly in setting priorities. Realisation of our weaknesses and limitations can enable us not only to empathise more deeply with others but also reawaken us to the love and concern of those around us. The urgent becomes subsumed by the important and the drive for recognition and status overshadowed by the desire to love and be loved. In our need we are drawn to put our house in order, to provide for those around us and to look more fervently to God's provision! Such changes of heart are a powerful witness to those who live for the moment without any thought of the future or their responsibility towards others. Recognising suffering as an opportunity to reach out to others, rather than a punishment, can free us to fully embrace our situations and be as Moses who,

> *'chose to be ill-treated along with the people of God*
> *rather than to enjoy the pleasures of sin for a short*
>   *time.*
> *He regarded disgrace for the sake of Christ*
> *as of greater value than the treasures of Egypt,*
> *because he was looking ahead to his reward'*
>   Hebrews 11:25,26

This is not to say we should look specifically for opportunities to suffer but rather that we should see our times of trial as opportunities to serve the Lord and to grow in faith through ways that are often not open to us.

Righteous suffering demonstrates the forgiveness of God

Finally, when innocent victims are able to offer forgiveness to the one who has caused their pain, it demonstrates in the most poignant way the forgiveness and love of God. In that display of compassion, the aggressor is shown that they can find reconciliation and peace with God, as well as with their victim. Phan Thi Kim Phuc came to the attention of the world when she was filmed in 1972, following a napalm attack, running naked out of her Vietnamese village, tears streaming down her face. Twenty-four years later, John Plumber, a pilot who helped organise the attack attended a Vietnam memorial service in an attempt to make peace with his past. At that service Phan Thi Kim Phuc spoke saying that she was not bitter and that even though she still suffered from the burns, she forgave the men who had bombed her village and murdered her family. John went to her afterwards to confess and express his deep sorrow. She placed her arms around him, and hugging him tight said, 'It's all right. I forgive you.' From that moment, he experienced a deeper peace than he had ever known before.

I am not suggesting that these opportunities to share our faith are sufficient explanations for all our suffering, but through trials, I do believe, God is able to use us powerfully in the lives of others, calling them to faith, bringing them hope and peace, and helping them to deepen their relationship with the Lord. In this way even our deepest struggles can become a source of life and hope to others.

The day of judgement

Recognising that God, in his mercy and forbearance, often leaves sins unpunished (Romans 3:25) does not mean that God will never judge those who rebel against him and attack the innocent and vulnerable. God has set a day when all will be judged and held accountable for all the things they have done, whether good or bad (2 Corinthians 5:10). This is the Day of the Lord, when Christ will return and his throne will be established forever. At that time Jesus says, the righteous and the wicked will be separated as a shepherd separates the sheep from the goats.

> 'He will put the sheep on his right and the goats on
>   his left.
> Then the King will say to those on his right,
> 'Come you who are blessed by my Father;
> take your inheritance, the kingdom prepared for you
> since the creation of the world...
> Then he will say to those on his left,
> 'Depart from me, you who are cursed,
> into the eternal fire prepared for the devil and his
>   angels."   Matthew 25:33-34, 41

On that day there will be no more opportunity to reflect on the suffering of the innocent, to reassess one's priorities, or to receive forgiveness and peace. It will be a day of reckoning when God will judge all according to the measure of grace bestowed upon them. To those who have received God's mercy there is the promise of eternal life with God, but for those who, throughout their lives, have continually rejected his love and inflicted pain and suffering on others, there is only the prospect of eternal separation and despair.

If you have spent your life wandering from God, rebelling against him or denying him, consider now his love for you in sparing you from judgement to this day. God is not willing that you should perish and spend eternity without him. He has been gentle with you, not treating you as you know you deserve. You have seen the suffering of others and thought nothing of it; you believe you are in control of your life and you do not need God to help you. But, look around you and see those, who in your heart, you know are better than you, more accomplished, more deserving, wiser, stronger. If they are suffering, will you escape? Consider those, who despite their suffering have grown stronger in their faith and their love for the Lord. Does that not speak to you of a greater reality? Do you not envy those who can find peace even in the face of death? Think of those who are praying for you even now, perhaps those you have harmed or grieved in some way; can it be that they care more for your soul than you do yourself? Do not spurn this opportunity to cry out to God and ask for his forgiveness. Do not presume on God's kindness and patience, for he will not wait forever. Take this opportunity to seek after him and to ask him to make himself known to you. The Lord Jesus says, *'behold, I stand at the door and knock. If anyone hears my voice and opens the door, I will come in and eat with him and he with me'* (Revelation 3:20). Listen to him knocking at the door of your heart? Hear his words of invitation. The Lord says to all who have forsaken him, *'I know the plans I have for you, plans to prosper you and not to harm you, plans to give you hope and a future... you will seek me and find me when you seek me with all your heart. I will be found by you.'* (Jeremiah 29:11-14). The apostle Paul urges you, *'not to receive God's grace in vain. For he says, 'now is the time of God's favour, now is the day of salvation'* (2 Corinthians 6:1,2). Today, will you take hold of God's promises for your life?

If you are going through a time of great trial, feeling that you cannot bear any more, that you are sinking under the waves. Remember the words of your God, *'when you pass through the waters, they will not sweep over you. When you walk through the fire you will not be burned'* (Isaiah 43:2). Remember also, that as great as your suffering undoubtedly is, equally great is your opportunity to witness to the goodness of God. Your struggles to find answers will in time become the bedrock to your testimony of faith and the reason why others will take your words seriously - for you are wrestling with giants and you will come forth glorious, as gold (1 Peter 1:6-9). Remember the word of our Lord to forgive those who persecute you, for in so doing you show them the love of God and their need of a saviour. Pray for them that through your witness they may come to faith and so be spared the day of judgement. In all that you do hang on to your integrity and cling to your faith in Jesus for in due time the Lord will raise you up, even as you put your trust in him. Therefore, *'fix your eyes on Jesus, who for the joy set before him endured the cross, scorning its shame... consider him who endured such opposition from sinful men, so that you will no grow weary and lose heart'* (Hebrews 12:2,3).

CHAPTER 10

Christ's Story and Our Story (Job 29:1-31:40)

His story is a point of connection, a merging of the ways, a promise of shared experience, a companion in fear and doubt and a friend promising salvation.

We have seen that God can use suffering to draw people to himself and deepen their walk with him. We have also observed that righteous suffering can be a powerful witness to those who have turned from God. These thoughts may have helped you to gain some further perspective in your struggles. However, there are still questions, one of which must surely be, 'where is God in my suffering?' This has been Job's constant cry as he has strived to understand his suffering, and as we reach the end of Job's words, we find him once more recounting his story, pouring out his complaint and protesting his innocence.

Job has re-examined his situation over and over again, exploring every detail in an effort to understand why God should abandon him. Convinced of his innocence, he has dismissed the arguments of his friends and believes God has unjustly targeted him. In his struggle to find answers, his eyes have been opened to see, by faith, some of the great truths of the gospel. He has come to realise he has an advocate, whom God has appointed, who lives to intercede for him and who is his most loyal friend. He has come to recognise that God has appointed an unimpeachable witness, to affirm his testimony and make representation for him. By faith he has called upon God to pay the price of his ransom and he has become convinced that God will redeem him and that one-day he will see his redeemer, face to face. However, like so many who hear these wonderful gospel truths preached from the pulpit, his renewed joy and faith is quickly submerged under waves of sorrow and dashed against the rocks of painful reality. Where is God in the storms of life? Why doesn't he answer my cry for help?

There was a time...

In his last words Job rehearses his final testimony to the God who is unseen. He begins by grieving the loss of the life he once had, a time when *'God watched over me, when his lamp shone upon my head and by his light I walked through darkness'* (29:1,2), a time when *'God's intimate friendship blessed my house'* (29:4), a time when *'the almighty was still with me and my children were around me, when my path was drenched with cream and the rock poured out for me streams of olive oil'* (29:5,6). Job grieves the loss of a time when he was respected in the city, spoken well of in the highest places (29:7-11); a time when he 'rescued the poor who cried for help, and the fatherless who had none to assist him' (29:12), a time when as Job says the 'man who was dying blessed me; I made the widow's heart sing' (29:13); a time when he upheld the rights of the weak and the needy, and when he broke the power of the wicked (29:13-17). He believed he would live long and spend his days in peace and comfort, with others hanging on to his every word. 'But now...' Two little words that carry so much pain and suffering. 'But now,' everything has changed. Even those at the very bottom of society, the dregs whom nobody cares about – those outcasts who have made no contribution to the lives of others, have risen up against Job. He laments, 'their sons mock me in song; they detest me and keep their distance; they do not hesitate to spit in my face' (30:9). They throw off all restraint; they strip him of all dignity (30:10,11). They lie in wait for him; they persecute him and make his life a misery (30:12-15).

We'd like to think that Job's story was unique, but sadly such tales seem all too common. Thugs endlessly tormenting a young man with learning difficulties until he dies; reckless youths urinating on war memorials and vandalising property; vandals smashing shop windows and looting; the elderly left to die alone in hospital; servicemen sent emails saying 'you are no longer required.' People who in earlier times have given all, for neighbour and country, but who are now an embarrassment, the butt of jokes and their contribution disregarded. One of the reasons many of us fear old age and infirmity is the loss of our significance, the loss of the life when we walked in sunshine of God's love, when we had the blessings of strength, vigour and beauty. We fight against it, struggling to hold back the tide of old age, but it creeps ever closer. We fear going out at night onto the streets, where once we played with carefree abandon; we fear for our children; we fear for our future. Job cries out that his life is ebbing away and that he feels as though God is grasping him by the neck of his clothing, twisting it tight and then throwing him into the mud (30:16-19). It's a picture of total abandonment and confusion, as Job calls out in vain to God, *'Surely no one lays a hand on a broken man when he cries for help in his distress,'* (30:24). He feels like a beggar lying in the road and God is walking past, not simply ignoring him but mocking his distress. Why is God treating him in this way? Did not Job weep for those in trouble and grieve for the poor?

...why doesn't someone hear me?

In a last plea Job puts forth his defence as a man of integrity and blamelessness, arguing that if he has ever done something wrong, may he be punished, but to his mind and conscience he has walked in the ways of God's laws all his life (31:1-34). In final desperation he cries out, *'why doesn't someone hear me!'* (31:35). At the start of our study of Job, I invited us all to sit alongside Job as he has poured out his heart, and to journey with him in his quest to find answers. I pray that at many points you may have discovered an affinity with Job, even a soul mate – one who understands what you are experiencing and with whom you can share your story. I pray that as you have listened you have been encouraged that here is a man who is not afraid to say what needs to be said and to confront those issues that are all too often swept under the carpet, for above all else we desire an authentic faith – not one which blindly follows, closing its eyes to tragedy and injustice whilst joyfully proclaiming a God who saves. I pray you have been emboldened to cry out to God, 'Why don't you hear me?'

As I reflect on Job's story, I'm reminded of the Lord Jesus, who came amongst us like a breath of fresh air, like the morning dew in a drought. He associated with tax collectors and sinners; he healed the sick and raised the widow's son; the people marvelled at his words and spoke well of him, even the religious leaders fell silent before him. On Palm Sunday they followed him rejoicing into Jerusalem, praising God and declaring him their champion. Yet, within a week those same people cried out for his crucifixion. They watched him stripped and beaten and nailed to a cross. They mocked him and spat in his face and called him accursed. Like Job, Jesus cried out in his dereliction, *'My God, my God, why have you forsaken me?'*

Job's story and Jesus' story

The story of Job is in part a foreshadowing or anticipation of the coming of the Lord Jesus. In Job we glimpse a revelation of our righteous Saviour, enduring the malice of Satan and the punishment of hell for us. Even more than Job, the Lord Jesus knew intimate fellowship with God as the Son of God, in eternal loving communion. Like Job, he experienced the alienation of God and the hatred of wicked men though he was blameless and without fault. As with Job, he was despised and rejected because of his sufferings. When we look at Job we are presented with a messianic portrayal of Christ such as we see in Psalm 22 or Isaiah 53, as God prepares us through the revelation of the Old Testament for the coming of our Lord. In Job, we have, God in Christ perfectly identifying himself with our humanity, as the apostle Paul writes of Jesus,

'who, being in very nature God,
did not consider equality with God something to
be grasped,
but made himself nothing, taking the very nature
of a servant,
being made in human likeness.
And being found in appearance as a man,
he humbled himself and became obedient to death
— even death on a cross!' Philippians 2:6-8

When Job cries, 'where is God in my suffering?' God's answer is 'right by your side!' When he cries out 'why don't you hear me?' God says 'call him Immanuel, God with us' (Matthew 1:25). His story is intimately entwined with Job's. Even more gloriously, we are to understand that the entirety of Job's life, as presented to us, from his times of great blessing and favour to his present suffering and desolation, finds its ultimate meaning and purpose in the life of Christ and God's story of salvation. If we want to have a definitive answer to the suffering of Job, it is that the revelation of Christ's passion may be made known to the world to the glory of God. Job had to suffer to point us to the suffering of the Christ, and as we shall see, Job was raised up and restored to direct us to the resurrection and ascension of Christ. Moreover, we are to understand that just as Job's life finds it's meaning in the revelation of Christ, so in the life of Jesus, Job finds his redemption and salvation. The lives of Job and Jesus are so interwoven that as the former reveals the latter so the latter redeems the former.

Jesus' story, our story

This understanding has enormous implications for us in our suffering, for just as Job's life can be said to prefigure that of Christ, so too, our lives find their meaning in looking back to our Lord in his death and resurrection; our story becomes intimately interwoven with Christ's story, and Job's story. As we have identified with Job in his struggles, weeping with him, sharing in his outrage, so too we find ourselves not only in dialogue with Job, but also in sweet communion with our Lord. As we take up our cross and walk in the footsteps of our Lord, experiencing his desolation and rejection so we come to know Christ and the power of his resurrection (Philippians 3:10,11). This is what our God intends, for he sent his one and only Son into the world to live among us that he might share our stories, and to die for us and rise again, that we might become one with him and his story.

These thoughts are captured in the poem 'Footprints,' by Helen Steiner Rice, which has comforted many people during times of severe trial. It speaks of a man who in a dream, looks back over his life as a journey along a sandy beach. He sees two sets of footprints indicating himself and the Lord walking side by side. However, there are times, the most difficult times, when he sees only one set of footprints in the sand. Like Job, he questions why the Lord should abandon him in his time of need. In his dream, God replies that it was during these times that God carried him. In this poem we see firstly, the Lord and the man walking side by side, so that in a sense we cannot tell whose journey the man is looking back over – it is his, but it's also the Lord's. In the same way in our lives, when we walk with the Lord, we are following his path, walking in his footsteps, as much as our own. Secondly, in the imagery of the Lord carrying the man through the most difficult times of his life, we glimpse a vision of our redemption and we hear afresh the words of our God, *'I have made you and I will carry you; I will sustain you and I will rescue you'* (Isaiah 46:4).

Therefore, we see that in Christ, our story and his story become one glorious history of salvation through suffering; our lives interwoven with his life so that as we are united with him in his death so we become one with him in his resurrection. We can perhaps picture this in terms of a tapestry fabric on which is imprinted the life story of our Lord. Our lives then become so many coloured threads that are to be woven into the fabric, each at their particular place, thereby bringing that part of Christ's life, death and resurrection into bold relief. As yet, we see only a few threads, those of our friends and neighbours, partially interwoven with ours, yet, each life, each thread, as well as reflecting the times of joy, success, blessing and peace we have experienced, also displays just as many occasions when we have known grief and sorrow, trouble and hardship. In this tapestry that is even now being woven, each life is left uncensored; each thread uncut, so that, as it is woven together with Christ's story, not just our happiness, but all our hurt and despair is there for all the hosts of heaven to see. We might find this an uncomfortable thought, for we spend so much of our lives hiding our hurts, but it's precisely these that most display the glorious story of our redemption in Christ. Your suffering and mine, far from being something to conceal, add a depth and a beauty in Christ that we would never have dreamed possible, like discovering a vein of gold in a shattered rock!

We suffer alongside our Lord

In our exploration of suffering, we have witnessed Job's abandonment and heard Jesus' cry of dereliction from the cross, so let us not be surprised if at times we too, feel as though we have been cast off by the Lord. The apostle Peter encourages us, *'do not be surprised… as though something strange were happening to you'* (2 Peter 4:12). Following his resurrection, we find our Lord walking alongside his despondent disciples on their way to Emmaus, having to explain to them that the Christ, first had to suffer before entering into his glory. They felt alone, bemused, abandoned – yet their hearts were strangely warmed by this stranger's words. It was only afterwards at the breaking of bread, that their eyes were opened and they beheld their risen Lord (Luke 24:13-35). It has been the testimony of many Christians that when they have asked for prayer, they have felt lifted up and carried through their trials. They will say that although the trial itself did not go away, though they could not see Christ in their darkness, yet they were made aware of his presence; they felt an abiding strength, a peace, a heart warming that came upon them, assuring them and enabling them to go on. It is this appreciation that in our suffering we are wedded to our Lord that is so important. In our communion service, we hear the words of our Lord, 'this is my body given for you, my blood shed for you.' They are an invitation to enter into his suffering, his brokenness and his abandonment that we may find his life, his joy and his peace. It is then as his life and death become entwined with ours and our stories become one that we find our hearts strangely warmed as his Spirit of grace and mercy and love flows into ours.

CHAPTER 11

God is Just (Job 32:1-37:24)

'Why me?' I cried out in my despair. 'Who am I that you should single me out for suffering?' The silence echoed around me. I felt so alone in the dark.

I stepped out and gazed up at the heavens. I felt so small, so insignificant.

'Why me?' I cried out in wonder. 'Who am I that you should single me out for love?' Peace and quiet enfolded me. God's light pierced my darkness, proclaiming 'I am with you.'

Before continuing, it is important we remind ourselves of mankind's essential problem in terms of our relationship with Almighty God, namely that all humanity is living outside the Garden of Eden, and consequently excluded from God's intimate presence. Although we have seen that, in his mercy, God showers us with his love each and every day, still we are living under judgement, alienated from God without any hope of heaven. Despite this, mankind can and has become blind to the situation, adapting to live within the confines of this world, as a prisoner comes to terms with his cell, or the oppressed learns to bear without dissention the unjust restrictions imposed upon them. As a result, individuals and nations valiantly endure the rule of Satan and the struggles that life brings, without a murmur, regarding it as our lot in life, the hand we have been dealt with. We simply accept God's love when it comes, unbidden and undeserved, as chance, a bit of good luck. Outside the garden, all our good works are as rags, and yet we live under the accepted golden rule that 'those who do right will be blessed and consequently go to heaven.' We believe that because in general our lives are comfortable and happy, our lives are blessed, and so we believe we will be similarly treated in the afterlife. But present fortune has no bearing on future grace. Time and again Jesus exploded this myth, with his parables of the 'Foolish Farmer,' (Luke 12:13-21) and the 'Rich man and Lazarus' (Luke 16:19-31). God is not willing that we should remain in this state and so he is constantly seeking to open our eyes to our situation and to provide the means by which we can be restored to him.

It is at this point that we are introduced to Elihu, who appears to have been sitting quietly alongside Job and his friends all the while, listening to their often-heated disputations. To some extent Elihu understands and sympathises with Job's situation, but he believes Job is so fixated on his suffering, insistent about his righteousness (33:9-10) and upset about God's refusal to answer his protestations that he is, albeit unconsciously, accusing God of injustice. Job is in danger of putting himself above God and making God somehow answerable to him. Elihu, therefore intends to reassert God's justice and reveal to Job the magnanimity of God, in that despite mankind's insignificance and ungratefulness, God is benevolent, attentive and just in all his dealings with his us.

God speaks to us

Elihu begins by addressing God's apparent silence, informing Job that contrary to his opinion *'God does indeed speak – now one way, now another, though man may not perceive it'* (33:14) and he offers two contrasting illustrations to support his conviction. He argues that God speaks through dreams, through the stirring of our conscience, *'in a vision of the night, when deep sleep falls on men as they slumber in their beds, he may speak in their ears and terrify them with warnings'* (33:15,16), and through suffering,

> *'a man may be chastened on a bed of pain*
> *with constant distress in his bones,*
> *so that his very being finds food repulsive*
> *and his soul loathes the choicest meal.*
> *His flesh wastes away to nothing and his bones,*
> *once hidden, now stick out. His soul draws near to*
> *   the pit,*
> *and his life to the messengers of death'*
> Job 33:19-22

God's reason for speaking in these ways, Elihu suggests, is to warn and deter individuals from doing wrong or becoming overly proud, so that they forsake God, who loves and cares for them. Indeed, Elihu insists, God does all these things to spare people from spiritual death, *'to preserve his soul from the pit,'* (33:18) and *'to turn back his soul from the pit, that the light of life may shine on him'* (33:30).

Martin Luther made a vow to become a monk, when a bolt of lightning knocked him to the ground. He saw this as a sign from God that the path he was walking would eventually lead to his destruction, unless he amended his ways. Later, he spoke of his journey to faith:

> *'My conscience became so disquieted as to start and tremble at the stirring of a wind blown leaf. The horror of nightmare gripped my soul, the dread of waking in the dark to look into the eyes of him who has come to take my life'* [1]

Many Christians can testify to having a similar experience, whereby they feel compelled to change their behaviour or even alter the whole course of their lives. In that moment they believe most fervently that God is speaking directly to them. Less common is our recognition that God may speak to us through specific illness or suffering. Yet some people, lying at death's door and being confronted with the prospect of hell, have given their lives to Christ, and then made a full miraculous recovery, going on to joyfully serve the Lord for many more years. God is very aware of our alienation from him, even if we are not! As Job has already discovered, Elihu affirms that without a mediator, someone to pay our ransom, all people will come under the judgement of God. Since even righteous Job only began to consider this seriously through this time of suffering, we should not be surprised that God should use suffering to shake us out of complacency. It may seem harsh and invasive of God to interfere in our lives in such a direct way, but as a parent cannot stand by and see his child run into danger, so God cannot turn a blind eye to our predicament. We settle too easily for the fleeting pleasures of this world; we cling to success, to money, to status, to whatever idol seems attractive, just like the Israelites of the past - and God has to woo from such things, because they distract us from him and the salvation he offers.

God is impartial

Elihu goes on to assert God's impartiality when it comes to justice. It was widely believed that God established individuals in positions of power and consequently, such people must be in his favour and belong to his 'inner circle.' But Elihu points out that when it comes to justice, God does not discriminate between the rich and poor or the powerful and vulnerable. He values all equally and is not slow to condemn those who abuse their authority or denounce those who rule unwisely, even if they are kings!

> *'is he not the One who says to kings, 'You are worthless,'*
> *And to nobles, 'You are wicked,'*
> *Who shows no partiality to princes*
> *And does not favour the rich over the poor,*
> *For they are all the work of his hands?*
>
> Job 34:18,19

Elihu contends that God in his omnipotence has *'no need to examine men further that they should come before him for judgement. Without enquiry he shatters the mighty and sets up others in their place'* (34:23,24). God does not need to set up public inquiries or convene a supreme court to establish guilt for he knows all our deeds and he has all authority to punish wickedness and to acquit the innocent. However, *'if he remains silent, who can condemn him? If he hides his face, who can see him?'* (34:29). Should God decide not to pass judgement but to overlook an offence, who are we to question him or doubt his justice.

God is above us

Elihu points out the fallacy of Job's claim that he derives no benefit from living a godly life for, *'what profit is it to me and what do I gain by not sinning?'* (35:3). He urges Job to look up at the vastness of space and the clouds that pass serenely by above his head, unconcerned and unmoved by all that is done on earth; how much more is God indifferent to the ways of man,

> *'if you sin, how does that affect him?*
> *If your sins are many, what does that do to him?*
> *If you are righteous, what do you give to him,*
> *Or what does he receive from your hand.*
> *Your wickedness affects only a man like yourself,*
> *And your righteousness only the sons of men'*
> Job 35:6-8

We are filled with our own self-importance if we think that anything that we do on earth, good or bad, has any impact at all on the God of heaven. Nothing that we say or do either adds to or detracts from his glory. Therefore, what nonsense for Job to debate 'what does obeying God gain,' as if mankind is in a position to bargain with God or have him acquiesce to our wishes. Elihu continues his rebuke saying, such is man's arrogance, that whilst the people may cry out when they are in trouble, no-one actually worships God for who he is, the Creator, who delivers us from darkness and teaches us wisdom (35:9-11). In all his complaints about his suffering and the injustice of God in responding to his call, how has Job praised the Lord for his greatness and humbled himself before the one who alone has the power to punish and to save (35:13-16)?

God is gracious

Consider therefore, Elihu persists, the graciousness of God in that although he is mighty in power, he does not look down upon us or treat us as insignificant or unworthy of notice (36:5). By grace he involves himself in our lives, ensuring those who do evil come to nothing and upholding the rights of those who are afflicted; his eyes are constantly on the righteous and he establishes them on thrones with kings (36:6,7). There is no reason why he should do this, for in reality we are inconsequential blobs of star dust and our petty concerns are necessarily trifling before the one who brings out the stars in the night sky. It is all of his grace and mercy, for he loves all he has created. Elihu says that even when God has cause to punish men for their wickedness, still he shows undeserved mercy and compassion, for

> 'If men are bound in chains, held fast by cords of affliction,
> He tells them what they have done – that they have sinned arrogantly.
> He makes them listen to correction and commands them to repent of their evil.

> *If they obey and serve him, they will spend the rest*
> *of their days in prosperity*
> *And their years in contentment'*   Job 36:8-11

It is only if people refuse to listen and continue to sin in arrogance that they will inevitably receive the judgement they deserve (36:12). Consequently, Elihu urges, God is seeking to woo Job from distress (36:16) for he desires to spare him not to destroy him – as Job seems to think.

The majesty of God

Finally, Elihu reminds Job that God is exalted in power and awesome in wisdom, doing marvellous things to reveal himself to all people, that we might praise him and extol his work (36:22-33). God is Lord over all creation, and at the thunder of his powerful voice the forces of nature rush to do his bidding and all creation ceases its labour in awe of the one who holds all life in the palm of his hand (37:1-12). Such is the majesty and wisdom of God that, *'he brings the clouds to punish men or to water his earth and show his love'* (37:13); the forces of nature, which we deem so uncontrollable and devastating in power, are but his messengers sent to accomplish his perfect will and establish justice on earth. God can use them as he wills, either to punish or to bless, to convict of sin or to console in suffering. In closing Elihu points out to Job that

> *The Almighty is beyond our reach and exalted in*
> *power;*
> *In his justice and great righteousness he does not*
> *oppress.*

Therefore, men revere him,
for does he not have regard for all the wise in heart'
Job 37:23,24

God is so far above humanity in power, in wisdom, in majesty and righteousness that before him we are as nothing. Yet, God does not oppress us or impose his will upon us. He treats us with kindness and compassion, love and mercy. Although our petty quarrels and bickering are as nothing to him, yet he takes notice of our situations and acts to uphold the cause of the poor and the oppressed. He delights in all his creation and in love seeks to reconcile all people to himself, for he is unwilling that any should perish and be lost forever.

Relationship over obedience

The difficulty for those who have grown up in a Christian moral setting is the tendency to regard God's commands as a 'to do' list with the proviso that if it's not on the list then it's not required. Job's response to God has always been, 'Tell me what to do and I'll do it, but don't blame me for not doing what I'm not told.' However, true obedience comes from knowing what is required without having to be told. For instance, within a loving relationship, it is expected that desires, hopes and dreams will be shared and understood, so that the right flowers arrive at the right time, washing is automatically picked up and put in the washing machine and Paracetamol is administered with but a look at one's partner. It is the same in our relationship with God for he does not want us as slaves but friends (John 15:14-16). Job needs to repent because he has devalued the relationship God wants with him. Job understands his involvement with God in purely business terms, in which God is expected to reward him for doing well. Job has lived his life in pride and conceit. He is wealthy, respected and a man of considerable influence. He expects to be heard and his questions to be answered – even by God. Elihu has to strip away all Job's confidence, *'look up to the heaven and see... if you sin how does that affect God? If you are righteous, what do you give to God?'* Nothing. Why should God care about you at all?

Isaiah expresses the same thought in this way,

> *'Before God all the nations are as nothing;*
> *they are regarded as less than nothing...*
> *God sits enthroned above the circle of the earth,*
> *and its people are like grasshoppers'*
>
> *Isaiah* 40:17, 22

Before God, Elihu argues, Job is no different to any other person and certainly in no position to interrogate the Almighty. Who does Job think he is? Who does Job think God is? Job sees his involvement with God as an equal partnership in which he has kept his side of the bargain but God has renounced his in allowing Job to suffer. God sees his relationship with Job as one that is broken for he doesn't want a slave to do his bidding but a son to receive his blessing. Job's attempts to win God's favour are futile; you can't buy love, yet that is all Job knows how to do. Since God doesn't play along Job accuses him of injustice. Job cannot listen to God until all his efforts at self-vindication have failed. That is what is so sad, because despite his apparent insignificance Job is known and loved by God. All his attempts to be noticed are unnecessary and ultimately damaging in his relationship with the Lord.

God wants to give us himself

The same is true for us! All our righteous acts do nothing to ingratiate us to God. If anything they offend him for not only are they stained with imperfection but they also derive from a refusal to accept the righteousness freely offered in Christ. Our God does not gain anything from our godliness and he is unaffected by our sin. It is purely out of love that he has determined to save us through the death and resurrection of his Son. Although he is as high above us as the heavens are above the earth, so great is that love, that he does not despise us but looks tenderly upon us with compassion, yearning to lift us up and bless us with divine goodness so that we want for nothing. It is for this reason that he desires to 'woo' us from the distractions of this world, because the world can never give us what we most need, which is God himself. Abraham was commended for his faith because he sought the Lord and refused to be sucked into the empty vacuum of materialism,

> *'he made his home in the promised land like a*
> *stranger in a foreign country; he lived in tents, as*
> *did Isaac and Jacob, who were heirs with him of the*
> *same promise. For he was looking to the city with*
> *foundations, whose architect and builder is God'*
> Hebrews 11:9,10

This doesn't mean we are all to live like Bedouin tribesmen, but neither should we be so taken with the things of this world that we lose sight of God and the promise of heaven. God longs for us to put all our trust in him and not to cling to trinkets and idols that cannot save. The worldly blessings that are showered on the good and the bad are not worth fighting over – rather we should crave the spiritual blessings of God that are found only in Christ.

God permits us to suffer out of love for us

It is because he desires to spare us from judgement that he allows us to hurt and feel pain. Our sufferings are God's reminders that we should not get too comfortable in this world, but that we should strive all the more eagerly for the life to come. As our Lord says,

> *'Man does not live by bread alone,*
> *but by every word that comes from the mouth of*
>   *God,'* and
> *'Store up for yourselves treasures in heaven,*
> *where moth and rust do not destroy,*
> *and where thieves do not break in and steal...*
> *you cannot serve both God and money'*
>   Matthew 4:4,6:20,24

This is very hard teaching for it very firmly puts us in our place. We are used to thinking of ourselves as the very pinnacle of creation, god-like in power and authority. It is very humbling to acknowledge that before Almighty God we are of no account and have no legitimate claim to anything. We cannot demand anything of God or expect any special dispensations. All that we have received from God is purely according to his grace and mercy. The very fact that he notices us at all is testimony to his loving kindness and generosity! Although everything that we do is of no consequence to the one who reigns over all, still he takes an interest in our lives and he sends suffering, like showers of rain, to cause us to look up to him.

We could tell each other countless stories of people we know who have endured great injustice and suffered terribly - and we could weep together. We could and sometimes do criticise

God, blame him, walk away from him. We want answers, 'Why me? Why them?' The answer Elihu gives is 'because God loves us.' Our Lord cannot bear to see us throwing our lives away, living for the moment and giving no thought to the future, when we will all have to stand before him as judge (Hebrews 9:27). God does not want us to live a life of slavery either, trying to earn a salvation that will always be beyond our reach. He does not want us to live a life in fear of the future and guilt about the past. He wants us to trust him and to put our faith in him. He wants us to accept the sacrifice of his Son as a gift of love. It breaks his heart to see us suffer, but sometimes it's the only way we will turn to him. Suffering is God's way of calling us to run to him. True, many run away and never come back. But would they ever have stayed and accepted God on his terms? I don't know. The real question is 'What will you do?'

1. Bainton, R.H. (1959) Here I stand A Life of Martin Luther: Mentor Books, USA pg. 30

CHAPTER 12

God's Purpose (Job 38:1-15)

Elihu has argued forcefully that God is supreme and that Job is wrong to consider himself on equal terms with the Almighty. He has put forward some powerful arguments to prove that God is just in his dealings with us, demonstrating how God speaks to us through dreams and suffering to warn us from wrong choices and to bring us to repentance, that we might be spared judgement. He has talked of God's impartiality, bringing down the proud and arrogant, and lifting up the humble and poor, that he might have mercy on all. He has spoken of God's majesty and argued that the Lord continually acts in love and grace towards all people. In wisdom, God orders all his works of creation for our eternal benefit as a loving father provides for his children. Far from attacking Job mercilessly and refusing to acknowledge his distress, God has sought to speak with Job through his suffering and to bring Job into a deeper more fulfilling relationship.

Job sets himself up as judge

For Job, and perhaps for us also, these arguments still do not provide a satisfactory explanation for his suffering. It seems odd, even wrong, that God should use suffering as a way of reaching out in love to his people. Job has heard all the human arguments and for different reasons they have all, in his opinion, fallen short of what he wants to hear, namely a plausible, pertinent justification from God for his suffering. However, before we 'listen in' to God's response, it is important to recognise both Job's arrogance and ignorance in making such a demand. Firstly, as Elihu has already touched on, Job is putting himself centre stage, unconsciously setting himself up as judge of God. By demanding God provides an explanation, he is implying that he will listen to God's reasoning and then decide for himself on its validity. However, God has no intention of allowing himself to be judged by anyone. God is in heaven and man is of the earth, for as the heavens are higher than the earth so are God's ways higher than our ways, and God's thoughts higher than our thoughts (Isaiah 55:9). When my children were young, they would often demand to know why they had to go to bed at a particular time, why they couldn't engage in a certain activity, why they had to eat their greens and so on, to which the answer usually, eventually, boiled down to 'because I'm your father, that's why!' They were not in a position either to understand or to make stipulations on what was to be done. In the same way, God is our heavenly Father and we are his children and we are to pay him due deference by respecting his judgement.

Is God to be beholden to his creation?

Secondly, suppose God should choose to reveal his purposes to Job, and that he 'graciously' accepts God's reasons as being satisfactory! What about the next time Job or someone else suffers - will God have to go through the whole process again? Is the Creator forever to be beholden to the demands of the created? *'Does the clay say to the potter 'what are you making? Woe to him who says to his father, 'What have you begotten?'* (Isaiah 45:9,10). The manager of a global company is not expected to provide every member of his work force with reasons for his every decision. His purposes are taken on trust as ensuring the best outcome for all employees and stakeholders. How much more should Job trust God's purposes which in the past have always been for his blessing and benefit.

Our suffering is unique to us

Finally, the reasons behind an individual's suffering are usually many and varied. As Aslan says to Lucy in 'Prince Caspian,' "Things never happen the same way twice."[1] Just because two people happen to share the same experience doesn't necessarily mean their experience derives from the same cause or has the same intended outcome. Just as the same act of suffering can elicit different responses from different people, so it can also be used by God to achieve different ends and be permitted for different reasons. One size doesn't fit all. As every person is uniquely hand made by God, so the purposes behind our suffering are uniquely tailored to draw us to Christ and mould us in his image.

However, although we freely acknowledge that no two people and no two situations are identical, we quickly fall into the trap of evaluating one person's misfortune by comparison with the demise of another. It should not be assumed that every hurt, every grief, every painful situation that happens to a person derives from a particular childhood experience, psychosis, criminal behaviour or with whatever other condition the world likes to label people. Neither should it be presumed that God's intended outcome of a situation would be the same for all people in all circumstances.

In western society, we continually jump to the same universal conclusion to explain a particular difficulty – and that conclusion often involves assigning blame to someone. We see this explicitly in the case of Job's friends, who cannot see any other explanation for his desperate situation than the presumption of sin. Jesus' disciples assume that either the blind man or his parents must have sinned for him to be born blind, until the Lord points out that his condition was to enable the work of God to be done in his life (John 9:1-3). Our modern world is in the grip of a culpability culture so that whether it is a car accident, or AIDS, or a natural disaster such as a tsunami or hurricane, some blame must be attributed to someone. In all these cases, such blanket judgements are rarely helpful pastoral responses, as we have seen, and neither do they lead us into a deeper understanding of the purposes of God.

Job's situation is a relationship to be healed

God is under no obligation and has no need to answer Job's queries, no matter how important Job may feel them to be, nor does God need to justify any of his actions. However, God is love and he mourns over our suffering and cannot bear to see us unduly distressed. Consequently, he graciously reaches out to us in ways that we can understand and from which we can receive comfort. He doesn't try to belittle Job's intelligence or pour scorn on his piety and integrity, he doesn't argue with Job over who is right and who is wrong. Instead, God draws near, effectively putting his arm around Job, and asks him a simple question 'Do you trust me?' In those few words, God encapsulates all Job's confusion, as if to say 'Job, you are righteous; you are innocent, yet you are suffering. I understand your bewilderment, but I'm not going to answer you in the manner you demand. Instead I want you to answer my question, "Do you trust me?" There are echoes here of Jesus' query to Peter following his denial of the Lord, 'Do you love me?' (John 21:15-19). God is passionate about relationship and more than anything else he wants to know, and he wants Job to know as well, that in all his circumstances Job loves and trusts God. This is much more relevant because Job's answer to this question will support him through every further trial he may encounter in the future, by establishing a deeper more grounded relationship with the Lord based on the experience of faith and unconditional grace rather than a blind intellectual assertion that God knows best. God is not treating Job's situation as a conundrum that is to be solved but a relationship that is to be healed.

God's museum

That's the issue God is addressing in this final discourse and to help Job, the Lord, as it were, takes him by the hand and leads him around the museum of God's creation. I remember as a lad often going to my local natural history museum in Forest Hill, called The Horniman. It's still there today, and just as fabulous.

It has several rooms or galleries, each with a particular theme, such as Woodlands or Tundra or Coastal environments. I used to love to visit and I'd spend ages just gazing at all the amazing exhibits - and I'd have my favourites as everyone does. Sometimes I'd just run round without really stopping to look because I'd become so familiar with the museum layout. I'd want to get to one exhibit in particular, just as one might quickly walk along a favourite path in the woods to get to a favourite spot. In my hurry to see the one exhibit, I often failed to see how the whole came together.

Similarly, when it comes to knowing God, we often seek out particular themes or favourite passages in the bible that we like to visit over and over, seldom taking in the whole picture of God's glorious majesty and holiness. Job's difficulty is that in his suffering, like us, he has been so focussed on his need that he has failed to see the big picture of God's awesome dealings with his creation. This is about to be remedied as God reveals his majesty to Job and to us.

I want us to visualize ourselves going round God's museum of creation, and listen as God reveals to Job each particular exhibit. By reflecting with Job on each illustration, I hope and pray we will each hear what God is endeavouring to say to us regarding suffering. In God's museum, like 'The Horniman,' there are a number of themed rooms, the first of which I have called 'New Beginnings' (38:4-15).

New Beginnings

I want us to imagine the Lord leading us with Job into an enormous auditorium, so vast that the walls, floor and ceiling recede into the distance. However, what grabs your attention is not the scale of the room, but the breath-taking vision of the earth, from its earliest origins, filling this enormous void. In awe you find yourself circling around it, gazing up at majestic snow capped mountains speckled with brilliant blue lakes and tarns; looking down upon dense green forests and vast swaths of desert yellow; marvelling at the vast unfathomable oceans, embracing the continents and islands alike with iridescent blue. Drawing closer, you can see the waves rolling effortlessly thousands of miles across the oceans to pound defiant cliffs, crash against rocky coastlines or lap peacefully along sandy shores. You see white cloudy pillars, like fleets of tea clippers, scud across clear blue skies, hear the sound of the wind howling through mountain passes, whilst gentle breezes whisper among woodland trees. You see everything uniquely made, uniquely being sculpted into something even more uniquely beautiful. You hear God's powerful voice whisper in Job's ear, *'Where were you when I made the earth in all its beauty and wonder? Who marked off its dimensions, who established all the laws of creation, the conditions for life? Who settled the earth at just the right distance from the sun? Who made the mountains and the valleys? Consider the universe - what other planet is like the earth, rich with abundant life? Imagine the sea bursting forth from the womb of creation. All that potential for life, all that power: who fixed its limits, who curbs its pride and governs the tides?'* As Job contemplates the beauty of the earth before him, he is aware of wisdom being at God's side in the act of creation,

> *'I was appointed from eternity,*
> *from the beginning, before the world began.*
> *When there were no oceans, I was given birth,*
> *when there were no springs abounding with water;*

before the mountains were settled in place,
before the hills, I was given birth…
I was there when he set the heavens in place,
when he marked out the horizon on the face of the
 deep,
when he established the clouds above
and fixed securely the fountains of the deep,
when he gave the sea its boundary
so that its waters would not overstep his command,
and when he marked out the foundations of the
 earth.
Then I was the craftsman at his side.
I was filled with delight day after day,
rejoicing always in his presence,
rejoicing in his whole world and delighting in
 mankind'

Proverbs 8:22-31

Wisdom, an allusion to Christ, the Word of God, was there from the beginning, observing and overseeing the work of his Father, continually rejoicing in his presence and delighting in seeing the earth take shape under God's loving hand. Wisdom was there when boundaries were set and laws were established so that the commands and purposes of God would be fulfilled. Wisdom was there when God separated the darkness from the light, the skies from the seas and the waters from the land; wisdom saw God fill the heavens with stars, the skies and sea with birds and fish and the land with all manner of vegetation and animals. Wisdom saw God create man and woman in the image of God and give them authority over all creation (Genesis 1) and wisdom saw that it was good. Through this vision of the earth, God is speaking to Job of how he formed and shaped it by the power of his word, brought light into the darkness and breathed life into emptiness. He is a God who takes that which is formless and devoid of life and transforms it, enriching it with his love and grace. God chose a barren rock and blessed it with life for the display of his glory; God chose an ordinary man named Abraham and blessed him with children, for the display of his glory; God took a nondescript nation, Israel and blessed them as the people of God, for the display of his glory, and God has chosen Job and made him the greatest man among the people of the East, for the display of his glory. The Lord is reminding Job that he has been chosen from the very beginning, that God has a vision for his life to bless him and to bring glory to God through him, and he says to Job in the light of this, 'Do you trust me?' Do you trust me to make your life beautiful, glorious, like the world you see before you?

Have you seen the sun rise?

God leans towards Job and directs his vision towards the East. He whispers, *'Have you seen the sun rise?'* Following his gaze, we see a warm glow spreading across the horizon, reds and oranges turning to golden yellow. The darkness scatters before it, shadows flee across the land, shrinking into crevices and scuttling under rocks. As the rays of sunlight kiss the earth, the features of the land, the hills and valleys, take shape, becoming visible and distinct; woodland paths that seemed so terrifying in the dark, become a place of delight in the warm sunshine; treacherous cliffs are transformed into majestic outcrops with inviting caves to explore.

> *'Have you ever given orders to the morning,*
> *or shown the dawn its place,*
> *that it might take the earth by the edges*

> *and shake the wicked out of it?*
> *The earth takes shape like clay under a seal;*
> *It's features stand out like those of a garment.*
> *The wicked are denied their light,*
> *And their upraised arm is broken'*

Job 38:12-15

The Lord speaks tenderly to Job, *'Have you seen all the wickedness that threatens the beauty of my creation. Have you witnessed all the darkness in people's lives because of greed, jealousy, hatred and vice? Each day I send forth the dawn to pierce the dark and to cleanse the land.'* God's speaks to Job of his unlimited patience, longsuffering and compassion. Through the sin of Adam, death has entered God's world (Romans 6:12-21), corrupting all that is good. Yet our God has not abandoned us, but taken upon himself the charge of redeeming the world in Christ. Until the Lord returns in glory to claim his own, we are given a picture of God's activity within his world, in which, each and every day, God starts afresh, picking up the pieces of our lives along our paths of destruction. He does not walk away from us, he does not punish us as he ought, but he shows us mercy, forbearing our sin however much it grieves his heart and damages the lives of those he loves. The innocent cry out and he will ensure they get justice but he cannot simply crush the wicked and wipe them from the face of the earth, for he is a God of mercy and forgiveness.

In his parable of the coming of the kingdom of heaven, Jesus speaks of an enemy sowing weeds among the wheat. The servant asks if he is to pull up the weeds, but the owner replies *'No, because while you are pulling up the weeds, you may root up the wheat with them. Let both grow together until harvest'* (Matthew 13:29,30). Often, in our times of suffering when we see those who are making our lives difficult flourish, it can seem as if God has turned a blind eye. In reality God is all too aware of our struggles but he is also concerned for others, who perhaps are weaker in their faith and who may be uprooted and lost if action is taken too soon. He therefore asks us to be patient and to trust him that all may be saved. As a powerful man will not raise his hand to a small child, no matter how much the tot may taunt and kick against him, so God is gentle with us, for he knows that we are but a breath, like the morning mist we are easily driven away by the first rays of the sun.

We must not lose sight of the hope before us

God has shown Job just two exhibits from this room of 'New Beginnings,' firstly the early earth in the hope that Job will understand that just as God took the dust and debris of a dying star, fashioning it into a beautiful world with the potential for abundant life, so he takes our beginnings, formed from stardust and makes us into the image of Christ, breathing his life into us. The earth's early history was chaotic and violent with meteor strikes, mass extinctions, ice ages, all the forces of nature unleashed in uncontrollable frenzy; volcanic eruptions, hurricanes, ball lightning, hail and sand storms, tsunamis and earthquakes. Other planets may have similar stories to tell, yet they are barren, mere objects of scientific enquiry. But under God's loving and purposeful hand the earth has been transformed into a world of great beauty, that is also a source of flourishing abundance to countless numbers of living species.

Reflecting on our earth's history, it is clear that our lives are likewise fashioned and shaped by our environment and the circumstances that befall us, not all of which are good. Many of

our beginnings are turbulent, confusing, even heart-breaking –
and without God's life-giving presence our lives would become
just like barren planets or burnt out stars, wandering through
an endless, lifeless universe. But God's touch, God's word,
God's breath transforms our emptiness into fullness and our
suffering into joy, bringing life and beauty into even our worst
beginnings, so that we become springs of hope offering eternal
life to others.

We are all born outside of Eden and so our lives from the
outset are less than perfect. Even our entry into the world
involves the pain of labour and the agonised cry of a new born
child, suddenly realising he or she has been cut off from the
source of their life. Yet, even before we cry, God hears us and
begins his work of grace in our lives – God takes that moment
of suffering to give us a new birth, a new life. We must all
pass through times of suffering on the way to becoming the
people we were ordained to be, but God wants Job and us to
realise that each period of suffering signals not an end to joy,
but a chapter in the story of our redemption. It is unrealistic
that we should not grieve for those things we have known
and now lost, but we should not lose sight of the hope that is
before us. We are being changed from one degree of glory to
another and with each step we must inevitably move further
from our old life to draw nearer to the one that is to come.
Our God cannot and will not leave us, for he loves us and he
has a glorious purpose for our lives. Therefore, he takes all our
times of trial, whatever they may be, and makes them all his
beginnings of grace.

God's light dispels our darkness

Secondly, Almighty God displayed the full glory of the sunrise that we and Job could catch a glimpse of how he works his gracious purposes into our times of darkness and despair. God wants us to understand that just as the breaking dawn dispels the darkness of night, so, day after day, the Lord patiently sends the light of his truth and mercy into our lives, to drive out sin and wickedness that we might be transformed into his likeness. God wants us to know that he is not distant, but intimately involved in all of our lives. Every day, the Lord enters into the drudgery of human existence. Like an attentive gardener picking up fallen leaves and removing slugs from lettuces or a faithful servant washing the grime from pots and pans and ironing creases from garments, God patiently and compassionately starts over, taking the mess of our lives and making them beautiful once more. God is not frustrated or wearied by all that is happening to us, but in thoughtful tenderness, he unpicks the tangled webs we weave, cleans up the mess we have made and repairs the damage we have done. God is not far away from any of us; every morning he sends his light to dispel the darkness and drive away the shadows in our lives. Each day, his pure light exposes wickedness and injustice, to destroy sin's power to corrupt and distort the truth (38:14,15). Every morning, he calls us to confess our sin and begin again, and through the power of his Holy Spirit, our struggles and stresses slowly begin to be transformed and take shape under the light of his gospel. His one pure light works uniquely in all our lives exposing sin, healing sickness, revealing truth, offering hope.

God is starting a new chapter in your life

Have you noticed all that God is doing in your life? Do you see how the Lord can take your present story and transform it into a new chapter? Do you realise the Lord is purifying and perfecting you for the glory of heaven? Your life is a bit like a building that the Lord is renovating and transforming into a temple fit for his Holy Spirit. There will be times when the Lord needs to take out a wall, relocate a bathroom or demolish a section in order to create an extension. Each alteration involves hardship and suffering but it is not a sign that God has forsaken you; on the contrary it demonstrates that God is actively starting a new project to make you more like Christ. For this reason James says, *'consider it pure joy when you face trials of many kinds,'* for the Lord is making you mature and complete (James 1:2-4).

Think for a moment about your new beginnings. Perhaps you are starting a new job, emigrating abroad, preparing for married life; perhaps you are going through a painful divorce and trying to make a new life for yourself; maybe you are saying goodbye to a loved one or welcoming a new addition to the family; you might be facing the prospect of retirement, having to accept disability or feel you have been given a new lease of life. In all your new beginnings, can you see God's hand at work? Do you glimpse his plan for your life? Will you trust him?

On Good Friday, the cries of 'Crucify him,' echoed loudly in the ears of his disciples, as they struggled to understand all that was happening. How could God allow this atrocity? Everything seemed dark, as black as the skies over the cross where our Lord was crucified. Everything seemed lost, devoid of hope and joy. Yet, God took all the darkness, emptiness and despair and turned it into joy, light and fullness with the dawn of Easter Day. Voices were raised in jubilant celebration, 'He is risen!'

A new dawn, a new hope, a greater victory and a new life await us all. Only let us believe. Let us take God's hand and allow him to lead us around his exhibits, to see the wonders that he has done, and to capture a sense of the vision and purpose God has for your life and mine. God is not distant, he is not cold towards you. He is right here with you and you are right there in his heart. He knows you are suffering, but he wants to start a new chapter in your life. He knows you want answers but he whispers to you today, in the light of all he has shown you, 'Do you trust me in your suffering?' 'Do you trust me to turn your time of trial into a new joyful beginning?' In the next chapter we find the Lord leading Job into another room of his museum of creation that he might be taken even deeper into his understanding of God's love for him and his world.

1. Lewis, C.S. (1990) Prince Caspian. Lion: Harper Collins Publishers: London. pg 125

CHAPTER 13

God's Sovereignty (Job 38:16-38)

In the previous chapter, we saw God lead Job around his museum of creation, taking him first into the auditorium entitled 'New Beginnings.' The Lord revealed to Job that he is there at the start of life with a glorious purpose for all of creation. God has a plan for each of our lives and he is able to take all our beginnings, even those born of suffering, and make them fruitful and beautiful. However there is still so much more that Job needs to understand about his relationship with the Lord, and so Almighty God takes him deeper.

Darkness and Light

In our minds eye we see the Lord escort Job into a second auditorium that has a chequered sign overhead labelled,

'Darkness & Light.' At the far end of this room, Job's eye is instinctively drawn to a huge dark cavern to which access is denied by two enormous black iron gates that tower overhead. No light comes from this cavern, it is totally black, devoid of all colour and blanketed in deathly silence. As he makes his way towards the gates, the Lord whispers, *'Have you plumbed the depths? Have you confronted the gates of death?'* (38:16,17). God asks whether Job has fully comprehended the darkness that lies before him and does he appreciate that all creation is under the same sentence. Everything that has ever been created must one day make its way to these gates – even the earth itself, which he has just gazed upon in awe and wonder. For as a result of sin, all creation is subject to decay (Romans 8:21) and will one day face destruction, *'the heavens will disappear with a roar; the elements will be destroyed by fire, the earth and everything in it will be laid bare'* (2 Peter 3:10).

Does Job have any understanding of what that means? Has Job walked the vast expanses of the earth to gaze upon every creature, every mountain, hill and vale? Has he considered their fate, watching every living thing grow old, die and fall into decay? Has he witnessed the very mountains erode, crumble and fall into the sea? We don't like to think about aging, or seeing loved ones pass away or discovering the places we loved to visit when we were young are no more. But God witnesses such things every moment of every day, for all things pass away but God is eternal, unchanging, the same yesterday, today and tomorrow. Does Job see with God's eyes, does he understand the despair of death? Does Job comprehend just how much these gates are an affront to the majesty of God? Does he appreciate his suffering within the context of final judgement? Can Job understand how much God wants to spare him from death, even if it means he must suffer for a time?

What is the way to the light?

As Job turns away from the gates, the Lord asks, *'Do you know where light and darkness reside?'* (38:19). He stands before a crossroad with well-worn paths fading into the distance, one well tended and broad, the other narrow and bordered by thorns and nettles. Which path should he take? He looks behind to find a maze of thousands upon thousands of such junctions, each one signifying a choice he has made in the past. He smiles as he sees himself choosing the righteous path more often than not. Sometimes, he recalls, the choice had been easy, but others times it had been almost impossible to choose the better way. He thinks about the hard times, like now, and remembers, particularly when faced with the prospect of suffering, he had often chosen the easier path. Sometimes he sees that was right, but as he looks back he recognises that often such decisions had led him down a convoluted cul de sac. He can see how he had to retrace his steps. Worse still, he sees himself straying towards those dark, forbidding gates, only to see unforeseen events pull him away. How can he know when to exercise caution and when to show courage? Has he ever really known which path would lead him to the Lord and which to the gates of death? Which path should he take now?

Job's desire has always been to dwell in God's light on his holy mountain, and to do that he has fervently strived to walk in the way of God's commands. He has always assumed that blessed is best, preferring the sunshine to the rain, yet does not hardship provide its own rewards as well? Living a righteous life does not mean a person will never walk through the land of shadow. How can he ever know if he is walking along the right path? Confronted with the gates of death and the mountain of his own ignorance, makes him realise that he has no idea how he is to come into the presence of God. He doesn't know where light and dark reside. Do we? In the thousands of choices we make each and every day, do we really know where they will take us?

Suddenly, before Job, a ray of brilliant white light pierces the blackness, illuminating his path to the right, like a shaft of sunlight breaking through dark thunderclouds. Job remembers the cry of the psalmist, *'send forth your light and your truth, let them bring me to your holy mountain, to the place where you dwell'* (Psalm 43:3). Conscious of his own darkness and ignorance, the light lifts him and gives him hope. He begins to understand salvation comes only through the gracious intervention of God,

> *'For God who said, 'Let light shone out of darkness,'*
> *Made his light shine in our hearts to give us the light*
> *Of the knowledge of the glory of God in the face of*
> *Christ,'* 2 Corinthians 4:6

Confidently he takes the path bordered with thorns and nettles, but shrouded in light.

God will lead us

God calls us to trust him because only he knows the way to his abode of light, only he can direct us along the right path. As Jesus affirmed to his followers, *'I am the way, the truth and the life. No one comes to the Father except through me,'* (John 14:6). He has wept as so many have refused his call only to find themselves at those black gates; he has witnessed too much pain, too much grief and despair and his heart is filled with so much love and compassion. Consider how many ways he has sought to lead us to himself, for he is aware of our ignorance, blindness and deafness to his truth. He has given us his commandments and provided us with teachers to educate us in the ways of righteousness. He has sent his Son as the Light of the World, to be our example that we might be drawn to him, as a moth to a flame. He has sent his Holy Spirit to remind us of Jesus' words and to guide us into all truth (John 16:12-15), promising, *'your ears will hear a voice behind you saying, 'This is the way; walk in it,''* (Isaiah 30:21). As a shepherd leads his precious sheep to still water and lush grass, the Lord promises to bring us safe to his pasture,

> *'My sheep listen to my voice; I know them and they follow me.*
> *I give them eternal life, and they shall never perish; no-one can snatch them out of my hand'*
> John 10:27

I remember as a child walking through East End Market with all its strange stalls, sounds and smells. I could easily have gotten lost, but I wasn't afraid because I had my hand tightly clenched in my dad's. I had every confidence in him for he knew the way to where we were going. That was all I needed to know! In the same way, God wants us to simply place our hand in his and to trust him for he knows the way to the abode of light and he will keep us safe even when we pass through the valley of the shadow of death (Psalm 23:4).

God has shown Job he is there in his beginnings and he is there at his end. He is the Alpha and the Omega; he has a purpose for our lives and he alone is able to bring it to full completion. He will illumine our path, guide us by his word and take us by this hand and lead us personally (John 14: 3) that we might arrive safe at his holy mansion. Will you trust him to guide you and keep you safe?

Sovereign Rule

Humbly, Job allows the Lord to lead him away from the gates towards another auditorium with the title, 'Sovereign Rule' emblazoned in gold lettering over the archway. On entering Job's ears are assaulted by the crash of thunder and lightning, of hailstones beating against glass windows, the thunderous roar of waterfalls, the cracking of glaciers and the howling of the wind. Inside, it is an enormous warehouse where all the elements of weather are stored before being deployed. In one corner he spies a huge mound of snow with flurries of snow flakes swirling and dancing above; in another hail is stockpiled in an enormous heap ready to be hurled upon the earth; lightning rods like glistening silver arrows are stacked neatly in another, whilst further away to the right, he can hear the sounds of many gales, winds and breezes tugging at their restraints. Speaking above the cacophony, the Lord begins to quiz Job,

> *'Have you entered the storehouses of the snow*
> *or seen the storehouses of the hail...*
> *what is the way to the place where lightning is*
> *dispersed, or the place where the east winds are*
> *scattered over the earth?*
> *Who cuts a channel for the torrents of rain, and a*
> *path for the thunderstorm,'*
>
> Job 38:22-25

What does Job know of these things? Can he call forth the wind and rain? Will the lightning do his bidding? Of course not and yet all creation is subject to God's sovereign rule, as the psalmist declares, *'He makes the clouds his chariot and rides on the wings of the wind. He makes winds his messengers, flames of fire his servants'* (Psalm 104), and through his gracious word all creation is blessed and flourishes. As Job gazes round he is struck by the awesome power of nature, the wind and rain; thunder and lightning; hail, ice and snow, all subject to God's bidding, wrecking havoc or bringing joy and blessing according to God's wisdom and design.

God delights in bringing life

The Lord continues, speaking of his attentiveness towards all his creation, explaining that he alone cuts a channel for the rain, to water *'a desert with no-one in it, to satisfy a desolate wasteland and make it sprout with grass'* (38:26,27). In his wisdom God sees what mankind does fails to appreciate; he cares for those parts of the earth that people have no knowledge of and no interest in. He quenches the thirst of the parched ground, that it may bring forth grass, even though there is no animal to eat it or person to enjoy it, for God delights in bringing life to that which is barren; his word does not return to him empty but accomplishes all that he desires (Isaiah 55:10,11). God's understanding and compassion are far, far greater than Job's. God sees the bigger picture and his concern is for all the earth and not just for Job in his tiny bubble of humanity. The Lord's design is not just to redeem the righteous in isolation but to liberate all creation from its bondage to decay (Romans 8:21) and to bring all things together under the gracious governance of Christ (Ephesians 1:10). Job's life is infinitely precious to God but it is still just one individual thread that is being patiently woven into the tapestry of God's work 'The Redemption of Creation.' Job thinks his suffering goes unnoticed, but God sees and cares for all his hands have made – even those parts Job himself, or anyone else for that matter, knows nothing about!

God is not about crisis management

The Lord continues asking Job if he knows who fathers the dew and the rain (38:28), who, as a mother, brings forth the ice and frost (38:29), signifying both God's authority and his creative power. He shows Job the many phases of water, the dew, rain, frost and ice that he has created to nourish our planet. In his wisdom, he alone holds them all in perfect balance and brings them forth at their proper time. Each is needed for the health of the land; the hard frost of winter to break up the ground that the soil may release rich nutrients for the coming spring; the April showers to bring forth the plants and the dew of summer to nourish tender shoots. So too, God is revealing to Job, that he uses all our circumstances together for our growth and nurture – times of drought and times of abundance, seasons of suffering and times of joy to break our pride, soften our hearts and quench our thirst that we might become even more fruitful, with the promise that *'those who sow in tears will reap with songs of joy. He who goes out weeping, carrying seed to sow, will return with songs of joy carrying sheaves with him'* (Psalm 126:5,6). God is gently informing Job that he is not about crisis management, turning up every now and again to patch up, restore order and keep things ticking over. Rather, God is watching over and intimately involved in every part of Job's life, the good, the bad and the indifferent, working all things together in accordance with his perfect plan, to bless Job and make him fruitful. Far from being unaware of Job's predicament, he is personally committed to him and will literally move heaven and earth to exalt him and save him. This period of hard frost in his life is but a prelude to the Lord preparing his heart for even greater blessing and fruitfulness. Yet there is still more than Job does not know!

Look to the heavens

Beyond the storeroom, God leads Job into a darkened annex that is bathed in a heavenly glow. Looking up, Job sees decorating the ceiling, myriad stars clustered in their constellations, shining in all their glory. The Lord points out to him just two or three heavenly arrays that Job will recognise, the Pleiades, Orion and the Bear. He asks Job if he has the power to bind the stars together in their constellations, to call them forth and to govern their individual motions through the universe,

> *'Can you bind the beautiful Pleiades?*
> *Can you loose the cords of Orion?*
> *Can you bring forth the constellations in their*
>   *seasons*
> *Or lead out the Bear with its cubs?*
> *Do you know the laws of the heavens?*
> *Can you set up God's dominion over the earth?'*
>   Job 38:31-33

God's power is awesome. Job is transported from the raw uncontrollable power of the forces of nature that dominate so much of life on earth to the peaceful unvarying, unhurried movement of the stars in the heavens. Removed from the hustle and bustle of every day life, Job witnesses the majesty and sovereignty of God writ large across the universe. There for all to see, the stars chart their way unerringly across the wide expanse of heavens in obedience to the universal laws laid down by their creator. Thousands upon thousands of galaxies, comprising millions upon millions of constellations of stars, all bound together by God's design and purpose, bejewel the night sky; each star unique and known by name. Invisible to the naked eye, each star has its own solar system with orbiting planets, satellites and asteroids. Throughout the whole of space every speck of dust, every planet, every star, every nebula and galaxy all exist by the will of God and move by the word of God. Job sees and understands so little of God's dominion and glorious purposes, so consumed has he been with his own little world. He knows nothing of the countless worlds God is creating every moment across the far reaches of space that no human eye will ever see. Similarly, he knows nothing of the acts of love and mercy God is even now bestowing upon men, women and children whom Job will never meet this side of heaven. God is doing wonders of which Job is entirely ignorant, miracles of grace that would humble him and silence his complaints forever if he did but know. As Job contemplates the vastness of space and his own insignificance he is forced to ask, 'Who am I that the Lord should notice me, let alone want to bless me and love me?'

It's a question we need to ask ourselves! There is no place in the entire universe where God's will is not fulfilled from the beginning of time to the end of eternity. In the midst of our earthly struggles the prophet Isaiah urges,

> *'Lift your eyes and look to the heavens: who created*
> *   all these?*
> *He who brings out the starry host one by one,*
> *and calls them each by name.*
> *because of his great power and mighty strength,*
> *not one of them is missing'*   Isaiah 40:26

Look up into the starry sky and see the vastness of the universe, the myriad of stars and planets, each one called and named by God, each one moving in obedience to his laws, each a sentinel in the darkness, testifying to the power and grace of God. It's easy to feel small and totally insignificant, easy to believe that our petty struggles are of no account to the awesome power of God and the majesty of his presence. Yet, like Job confronted by his own smallness, God declares to you and I, 'You are mine and I love you.'

God knows you by name

As we gaze up at the stars, some of which seem so bright they dominate the night sky, steadfast and sure they are used by sailors to navigate their way across the oceans, we may wonder whether we are shining lights for our God, showing people the way to truth and salvation. Too often, we may feel more like those stars that seem barely visible above our own man-made light pollution. In times of doubt and suffering, our light seems more like a faint flicker, rather than a sure safe guide to those seeking the Lord. Often, in such circumstances, we can feel ashamed and unable to share our faith or even to draw near to the Lord. Yet as each star is known by name and called by God, so the Lord would have us know that he has chosen us and he loves us still (John 15:16). He does not judge us on the quantity of our faith or how brightly we shine, but on the purity of our faith and the fact that we do shine, no matter how faintly. Indeed, it is in the darkest night that the faintest glimmer shines all the more brightly; so it is with our faith, which though it may be weak, is rendered more visible and distinct in times of suffering.

It may be that as you look up into the night sky, your eyes are drawn to the well known distinctive constellations, such as the Plough, the Pleiades or Orion. Bright and clearly visible in the northern hemisphere and yet the fainter stars in the clusters are often completely overlooked. It may be you belong to a thriving church and yet you find it difficult to shine for your light seems lost in the brilliance of those about you. Perhaps, you feel your contribution goes unrecognised and consequently your faith is not stretched. In times of suffering, when your light burns dim, you believe that no-one even notices, for you are but one small candle among so many powerful floodlights. In such situations, it is easy to believe that God doesn't see you either and that his eyes are only on the recognised leaders of the church. Yet remember God chose David over his eldest brother Eliab for the Lord does not look at the outward appearance but at the heart (1 Samuel 16:6-7), he chose Gideon though he was the least in the weakest clan of Manasseh (Judges 6:15) and the apostle Paul who by his own confession was the least of all the apostles (1 Corinthians 15:9). Take heart, the Lord sees you and in due time he will raise you up if you keep your faith in him.

Alternatively, like a lone star glimmering in the heavens, you may be a member of a small rural community with little Christian fellowship and because of that you feel overwhelmed by your calling to shine as a witness to the Lord. Remember the Lord's words to Abraham, 'Look up at the heavens and count the stars... so shall your offspring be' (Genesis 15:5). As the Lord called Abraham so he has called you; he is ready to bless you with many spiritual descendants, as numerous as the stars in the sky – only believe. Do not focus on your weakness but on God's greatness; not on your failures but God's promise; not on your insignificance but on God's love for you.

When we forget God's power it weakens our prayer life

In following the Lord and Job around God's museum, we have only just begun to scratch the surface of God's wisdom and love for all his creation. God is greatly moved by compassion when he witnesses the destruction of that which he has created in love (Psalm 103:13). Jesus wept at the grave of Lazarus his friend (John 11:35), his heart went out to the widow who had lost her only son (Luke 7:11-15) and he wept over Jerusalem for the people did not know what would bring them peace (Luke 19:42). God is not dispassionate and he is not distant: He is the God of all the living and he exerts his sovereign rule over all creation that it may flourish and grow, directing the forces of nature and controlling the elements to accomplish his loving purposes. All this God does for the benefit of his creation, even watering a desolate land where no one goes that it may have the joy of giving and sustaining life. So the Lord says to his people,

> 'Why do you say, O Jacob, and complain, O Israel,
> 'My way is hidden from the Lord;
> my cause is disregarded by God?
> He gives strength to the weary
> and increases the power of the weak.

> *Even youths grow tired and young men stumble*
> *and fall,*
> *but those who hope in the Lord will renew their*
> *strength.*
> *They will soar on wings like eagles;*
> *they will run and not grow weary,*
> *they will walk and not be faint'*
>
> Isaiah 40:27-31

Even the best of us, the strongest, those with the greatest faith, get tired and weary, but we should not lose heart for we all have God's eternal promise that those who put their trust in the Lord will be renewed, they will soar on wings like eagles, they will run and not be faint, for the Lord is able to raise them up and strengthen them by his grace.

The Lord has revealed to Job his wisdom in establishing the earth on firm foundations and the setting apart of the dark and the light. God has revealed his wisdom in his sovereign rule over the laws of nature, the weather and the motions of the stars in the heavens. God's unseen hand is over all to bring about his loving purposes. Can we order the world to our satisfaction? Can we command the weather? Can we direct the stars? We may know the laws of nature, but we have no real control over them! The great sadness is that in our ignorance we also deny God's power over his world, ascribing all of God's acts of mercy to an impersonal 'Mother Nature,' that has no conscience or concern for humanity. As a result, we often fail to recognise God's intimate involvement in our world and his longing to save us.

When we forget this and attribute God's activity in creation to 'Mother Nature' it inevitably weakens our prayer life, because it causes us to close our minds to miraculous power of Almighty God, revealed in response to the prayers of his people. Who parted the Red Sea at the command of Moses? (Exodus 14:21) Who made the sun stand still over Gibeon at the request of Joshua (Joshua 10:12-14) and retreat up ten steps on the stairway of Ahaz at the prayer of Isaiah? (2 Kings 20:11) Who withheld the dew and the rain, except at the word of Elijah (1 Kings 17:1) and caused fire to fall from heaven upon his sacrifice? (1 Kings 18:38) Who gave a son to the Shunammite at the word of Elisha (2 Kings 4:16) and caused the axe head to float? (2 Kings 6:6-7) Who calmed the storm and the waves? (Mark 4:37-39) Who cleansed the leper? (Mark 1:40,14) Who withered the fig-tree (Mark 11:20,21), fed the 5,000 (Mark 6:30-44), healed the sick (Matthew 4:24), gave sight to the blind (Mark 8:22-25), hearing to the deaf (Mark 7:31-35) and raised the dead? (John 11:41-44) Let us not say that God is limited by the laws of Mother Nature! Let us not believe that God does not answer the prayers of his children (Joshua 10:14; John 15:7-8, 16-17). The Lord says to us all, especially those who are suffering, 'Do you know the way to the abode of light? Do you know how to save yourself? Can you set up your dominion over the earth? Do you know that despite everything, you are God's child and precious in his sight?' And in your suffering, he asks 'will you trust me?'

CHAPTER 14

God's Compassion (Job 38:39-39:12)

It is a wondrous thing to contemplate that the God who created the heavens and fashioned man from the dust of the earth, should choose to reveal himself to Job, who by his own admission is but a wind-blown leaf (13:25). Yet, that is the nature of the God we worship, who desires to be in relationship with us. Job has stared up into the heavens at the vast array of stars and asked himself the question 'who am I?' and God has answered most emphatically 'You are mine.' Everything Job needs to know about his identity and his eternal security is tied up in knowing God as Father. It is for this reason, God has chosen to escort Job through his museum of creation, that Job might better understand God's wisdom and faithfulness to all he has created in love. His aim is to bring Job to the point where, even in the midst of his suffering, he can say, 'Father, I trust you.'

All creatures great and small

So far we have explored three aspects of God's providence, which we have envisaged as three rooms in God's museum entitled, 'New beginnings,' 'Darkness and Light,' and 'Sovereign Rule.' We have glimpsed God's wisdom in laying the foundations of the earth and witnessed his power and authority over the forces of nature. Now the Lord reveals to Job his compassion and concern for all living things by leading Job through a wide gallery entitled, 'All creatures great and small.' From the entrance the floor slopes gently upwards until, at length, the corridor opens to reveal an enormous ark in cross section, filled with every conceivable species of animal, bird, fish and insect that has ever lived. The ark is sub-divided into countless enclosures, each one providing a natural habitat for a vast variety of species and supporting its own ecosystem. From their vantage point God directs Job firstly to a savannah landscape where a pride of lions are contently dozing in the mid-day sun, and then to a forest woodland in which a family of young ravens are 'cawing' noisily from their nest high in the trees. The Lord turns to Job and asks,

> *'Do you hunt prey for the lioness and satisfy the*
> *hunger of the lions*
> *When they crouch in their dens or lie in wait in a*
> *thicket?*
> *Who provides food for the raven when its young cry*
> *out to God*
> *And wander about for lack of food?'*
>
> Job 38:39-41

The Lord reminds Job that it is he who satisfies the needs of every living creature; the strong and the weak, the great and the small, the good and those regarded as evil; those who are capable of hunting for themselves as well as those who are totally dependent on the support of others. Job surveys the ark, gazing in awe at the limitless variety of environments God has designed and created in love to meet the needs of all his creatures; desert plains to tropical rainforests, arctic tundra to prairie grasslands, mountain ranges to lowland valleys, deep oceans to shallow estuaries, coral reefs, sandy shores, rocky outcrops and deep sided canyons, every one brimming with life, overflowing with creatures of every kind, shape and colour. The words of the psalmist ring out in Job's mind,

> 'these all look to you to give them their food at the
>   proper time.
> When you give it to them, they gather it up;
> when you open your hand, they are satisfied with
>   good things
> When you hide your face they are terrified;
> When you take away their breath they die and
>   return to dust.
> When you send your Spirit, they are created,
> And you renew the face of the earth'
>
> Psalm 104:27-30

God is Lord of all. Lost in his suffering, Job has forgotten that all living creatures look to his heavenly Father for life. Whether they are young or old, many or few, ferocious or tame, all depend utterly and completely on God for everything they need to survive and thrive. In his wisdom and mercy God does not withhold any blessing, providing a niche for every single creature, without partiality, even as he provides a place for each and every person to live that they might seek after him and be satisfied (Acts 17:26). As Job surveys all the creatures flourishing within God's ark, he feels humbled that he has questioned God's knowledge of his situation. Yet how is he to understand God's care in the light of suffering?

God wants to be part of our lives

The Lord directs Job to some mountain goats leaping fearlessly around a lofty rocky outcrop and a herd of deer contentedly grazing on a grassy hillside. In a secluded copse Job notices a lone doe walking around, clearly in some distress. A proud stag stands by her, but makes no effort to draw near. He barks urgently and as if by some command the doe crouches and begins to bear down. Soon, a blood soaked foal appears, its head and front legs hanging awkwardly between her legs. A few tense moments later a healthy, albeit wobbly, colt is delivered and the mother collapses to the ground; contentedly she begins to lick her new born clean. The Lord whispers to Job,

> *'Do you know when the mountain goats give birth?*
> *Do you watch when the doe bears her fawn?*
> *Do you count the months till they bear?*
> *Do you know the time they give birth?'*

Job 39:1,2

The Lord speaks of how he watches over all his creatures, as a loving parent, counting the months till they should bear their young, watching over them as they give birth; observing the young as they are nurtured, following them as they grow up and leave the safety of home to become parents themselves (39:3-4). As Job gazes at the young foal, I picture him remembering the birth of his firstborn, marking off the days of his wife's pregnancy. Every week he and his wife would get out the baby book and imagine the various stages of her confinement; the development of the heart and lungs, the formation of the fingers and toes, the appearance of clear facial features, his nose, ears and even eyebrows. I imagine Job recalling their shared excitement of feeling their baby's first movements, conscious that he could now hear their whispered voices. I see him counting the days and the hours to their son's birth, wondering what it would be like to hold this miracle of life in his arms; remembering how immediately after the birth, he simply could not stop smiling. In Job's reflections, he begins to understand in a deeper way that God was there with them. He also was counting the days, sharing the excitement and the joy. He too watched Job's children grow up strong and become independent. In a flurry of emotion Job realises that God wanted to be part of their lives, just as much if not more than Job wanted his children to know God. The Lord had blessed him with such wonderful children because he knew that Job would love them and pray for them. In the same way God also shared Job's grief and pain. Job has been so preoccupied with his own grief that he has never stopped to ask himself what God was feeling! Job begins to understand that the curse brought upon the world through sin grieves God (Genesis 6:6) even more than creation groans (Romans 9:22). Every moment of every day his heavenly Father watches his creatures, labour and struggle in their pursuit of joy, wanting to take upon himself their hardship and pain, whilst they remain largely ignorant of his gracious provision. He begins to see that in this world, the joy of life is intrinsically interwoven with suffering; one cannot exist without the other.

Freedom and submission

Without a word, the Lord takes Job to see a wild donkey
grazing in the salt flats,

> *'Who let the wild donkey go free? Who untied his*
> *ropes?*
> *I gave him the wasteland as his home,*
> *The salt flats as his habitat.*
> *He laughs at the commotion in the town;*
> *he does not hear the drivers shout.*
> *He ranges the hills for pasture'*   Job 39:5-8

Job starts to think about the wild donkey's domesticated cousin.
He had owned 500 donkeys until the Sabeans attacked and
carried them away (1:14,15). He'd treated them well, providing
fresh hay, grass and the occasional carrot, but they were still
beasts of burden, expected to do the 'donkey work.' This wild
animal however, refused to submit to authority, and was set
free to roam wherever he pleased; he carried no burdens, he
cared not for orders. True he might often go for days without
food, ranging far and wide for good pasture, but that was the
choice the Lord had given him. As Job reflects on this he begins
to see that even his freedom is bound up with suffering, for
that is the price of his stubborn insistence on independence.

Finally, the Lord leads Job to a large herd of wild ox or aurochs,
peacefully grazing in an open plain. Job has never been so
close to these enormous animals; the most powerful of all
hoofed beasts, exceeded in size only by the hippopotamus
and elephant[1]. Now extinct, the aurochs symbolised strength
and power, and Job feels distinctly intimidated as he stands
beside them. This is not a creature that can easily be tamed:

The aurochs is truly wild and he does as he chooses. The Lord questions Job,

> *'Will the wild ox consent to serve you?*
> *Will he stay by your manger at night?*
> *Will you rely on him for his great strength?*
> *Will you leave your heavy work to him?*
> *Can you trust him to bring in your grain*
> *and gather it to your threshing floor?'*
>
> Job 39:9,11-12

Mankind may be able to domesticate a donkey, but there is no way he can tame the aurochs to do his bidding. Yet, by implication God says that this powerful animal willingly consents to serve the Lord and stay by his side (39:9). Rather than exercise his freedom and fend for himself this mighty creature submits to God's just and gentle rule, and in so doing finds true freedom and fullness of life.

God does not impose his will

His eyes opened, thoughts begin to crowd into his mind. Job starts to see his life within the context of the whole of creation, in which painful suffering and joyful abundance indissolubly coexist; the pain of labour coupled with the happiness of birth, and the death of one creature often inseparable from the life of another. Job has believed himself a victim, singled out by God for punishment, rather than viewing his suffering as that which unites him with all creation, in death and redemption, whereby they are together loved and cared for by the Lord and are being transformed by his mercy into a new heaven and new earth.

Job now recognises a fundamental difference in the nature of God's rule and man's. Whereas mankind tends to domesticate, God seeks to liberate. Humanity generally imposes his will upon animals either to use them for his own benefit or believing he knows what's best for them. Job has been guilty of assuming God similarly regards his people as pawns to fulfil his higher purposes. But God is not like that! He lets the wild donkey go free; he cares for the oppressed and exploited, the widow and the orphan. He liberates his people Israel from Egypt, by a mighty hand and an outstretched arm (Deuteronomy 4:34), carrying them on eagle's wings to a good land, flowing with milk and honey. God lifts the burdens from our shoulders and carries our sorrows upon his back that he might bring us into a spacious place (Psalm 16:5-6). God does not impose his will but respects our right to choose. He will not stand in the way of those who decide to reject his authority. As with the wild donkey, God grants them freedom and, in love and mercy, provides a spacious place for them to thrive. This inevitably leads to a degree of suffering both on the part of those allowed to go their own way and upon God who, as a loving parent, bears the full consequences of all their actions and decisions. God is not like Bildad portrayed him, quick to punish any indiscretion (8:4); he is gentle and compassionate abounding in mercy and love.

We are all interconnected

God has opened Job's eyes to see that each creature has a vital role and place within the single worldwide ecosystem that is creation. As each creature is unique, so is the habitat they occupy and God's gracious provision for them. To argue that one is more blessed than another is foolish, as is to imagine that each can live in total ignorance of the other. A parallel illustration can be seen in the Apostle Paul's description of the Church as a single body made from many interdependent parts, some of which are high profile, whilst others are weak or plainly embarrassing (1 Corinthians 12:12-26). Notwithstanding this, all members of the body are to be equally valued and of equal concern; *'if one part suffers, every part suffers with it.'* The Lord provides for each and every person, irrespective of who they are, whether a successful businesswoman in the New York banking sector, a poor farmer eking out a living in the wilderness of Niger or a beggar on the streets of India – all are equally loved and cared for by Almighty God, and all are to be treated with equal concern and validity. In his mercy God puts us in families and nations, providing us with work for our hands and food for our bodies that we might know that all life is dependent upon him: Similarly, we are to provide for each other as witness to our common humanity. Those who have been granted authority and power are to use their position to provide for those under their care, and God will hold such people to account, for the Lord calls the mighty to do his bidding; kings and princes to carry out his will (Isaiah 45:1-6). If they renege on the responsibility he has given them and oppress those under their charge, he is able lift up the humble and bring down the mighty, as we proclaim gloriously in the Magnificat, *'he hath put down the mighty from their seat and hath exalted the humble and meek,'* (Luke 1:52).

Do not focus or your wants but your need

Jesus speaks of God's provision and care for us all in his Sermon on the Mount, where he reminds us that it is our heavenly Father who feeds the birds of the field, and clothes the lilies of the field (Matthew 6:26-29). Consequently, we are not to be concerned about what we will eat or wear because our heavenly Father will provide lavishly for us. It is when we forget this that we begin to lose our trust in God, becoming either proud of our achievements (Deuteronomy 8:10-14) or envious of the riches of others. In our pride we cling to what we have gained, as if we had earned it rather than received it as a gracious gift from God to be used for the blessing of others. When envious of others, all we can think about is becoming rich for we see that as the answer to our need rather than the grace of God.

In either case, it is then but a short step to worshipping the gods of materialism and setting our hearts on those things that do not endure. As our Lord reminds us,

> *'Do not store up for yourselves treasures on earth, where moth and rust destroy, and where thieves break in and steal. But store up for yourselves treasures in heaven… for where your treasure is your heart will be also… you cannot serve both God and money'* Matthew 6:19-24

The inevitable consequence is that we begin to focus on our wants, or at least what society tells us we want, rather than our fundamental need. We begin to worry about our lives, how we will provide for ourselves and our family, our security, our health, our retirement, rather than looking to the Lord and seeking first his kingdom (Matthew 6:25-34). We become dissatisfied with our place in society, the disadvantages we observe in our situation and the level of support we feel is our right. We look down on those perceived as less fortunate than ourselves and often fail to recognise that the child growing up in the poverty and hardship of Somalia often seems to know more about joy and peace than the highly paid executive living in the luxury of Beverley Hills.

As a result, many dismiss the notion that God loves them, for they measure his devotion purely by the material benefits they receive. They pour scorn on the belief that God longs to be a part of their lives, to bless them with good things and to share their delight in receiving them. For such people God is a fraud who refuses to provide them what they want, like a mother who gives their child greens. Yet, the Lord loves to give us all great gifts, even the miracle of life itself, that we can learn how to be conscientious parents, entrusted with the responsibility of raising a child to know and love their heavenly Father. He may not always bless us with material gifts, but these are a cheap grace of no lasting value, though they may shine like gold for a while. There are much greater and eternal gifts that he wants to graciously bestow upon us. These are his continual presence, his one and only Son, whom he gave as an atoning sacrifice to redeem us from the power of sin and his Holy Spirit through whom we receive all the benefits of Christ's death and resurrection.

God gives us these gifts because he yearns to set us free from the ties of sin that bind us. He recognises more clearly than we do the consequences of our separation from him as people living outside of Eden. He understands that we are slaves to sin and face constant temptation by the world, the flesh and the devil, and he wants to deliver us that we may be brought into the freedom of his promised rest (Hebrews 4:1-11). He graciously invites us,

> *'Come to me all you who are weary and burdened,*
> *and I will give you rest.*
> *Take my yoke upon you and learn from me,*
> *for I am gentle and humble in heart,*
> *and you will find rest for your souls.*
> *For my yoke is easy and my burden is light'*
>
> Matthew 11:28-30

The question we must again each ask ourselves is, 'will I trust him?'

1. Andersen, F.I. (1976) Job. Tyndale OT Commentaries. IVP Leicester, England, pg.281

CHAPTER 15

God's Wisdom (Job 39:13-30)

Encountering God in his word often involves putting ourselves into the scene, posing our questions of the text and using our reflections to transform our thinking. As we walk with Job around God's museum of creation, you may already have begun to express your own thoughts to God through Job - and received answers. As we move deeper into God's revelation to Job, I have found it helpful to put myself in Job's place and ask some of those questions that I feel would have troubled him. I hope and pray that as you continue walking with Job, God will speak personally to you of his wisdom in your life.

The Ostrich

In silence, Job is led around the ark to look in from the other side, which is entitled 'Wisdom.' The first sight that greets his astonished eyes is an ostrich walking with purposeful strides, turning first one way and then another, in an entirely uncoordinated manner, as if looking for something she has lost. At her feet lay her clutch of eggs, thinly covered with sand, yet she seems not to notice. Unaware she might crush her young, she stomps heedlessly around in her pursuit of busyness, pecking in the sparse grass for seeds and roots. Job observes two newly hatched chicks desperately scurrying after their mother, but she pushes them away, seemingly annoyed by their interruption. The Lord informs Job that he did not endow the ostrich with wisdom or give her a share of common sense (39:17), for she

> *'lays her eggs on the ground and lets them warm*
> *in the sand,*
> *unmindful that a foot may crush them,*
> *that some wild animal may trample them.*
> *She treats her young harshly, as if they were not hers;*
> *she cares not that her labour was in vain.'*
>
> Job 39:14-16

As Job watches her fruitless attempts at motherhood, he reflects on his own parenting skills. His eyes fill up as he remembers precious times that are now gone, and finds himself angry at this bird for neglecting the opportunities given her. She gives no thought to the protection of her young and makes no plans for their nurture. She is too preoccupied, unconcerned or unaware that all her hard work may come to nothing! She has wings that she flaps joyfully but she lacks the ability to fly!

As she stomps perilously close to her clutch of eggs, Job steps forward, startling her. In a heartbeat she turns and races off, leaving her young unguarded.

'Do you see her run?' God says excitedly, 'a bird outrunning a horse!' It was true; her powerful legs carried her effortlessly across the savannah. For all her shortcomings, you could not but admire the incongruity of this wondrous creature. Job's eye is drawn back to the eggs lying unguarded on the ground. Job sees first one chick, and then another, break out of its shell and begin to step clumsily over the sand. Despite her carelessness, Job realises, God still blesses her with baby chicks and by his grace he is convinced they will thrive to become the largest of living birds.

He begins to understand that his heavenly Father, bestows the gift of children upon the poor, the disadvantaged, the weak, uncaring and ungrateful sinner as well as upon the wealthy, the privileged, the strong, loving and dutiful saint. God doesn't vet people as to their suitability for parenthood, withholding his blessing from those who fail to meet his criteria. We may live in a broken world but God doesn't treat us as broken people. He regards us, first and foremost as his children, and as a loving father, he continually seeks ways to encourage and challenge us, giving us more responsibility, even if we are undeserving, so that we have the opportunity to grow in maturity and wisdom. He also sees that whatever the family background, privileged or poor, loving or indeed abusive, the Lord is able to cause his children to flourish.

The Horse

In a neighbouring habitat, Job sees a powerful black horse cantering majestically across an open field, his dark flowing mane catching the breeze. The Lord questions Job, *'Do you give the horse his strength… do you make him leap like a locust… rejoicing in his strength?'* (39:19-21). Sensing Job's presence, the horse immediately turns and trots confidently over, coming to stand just a few inches away. He towers over Job, who sees his muscles quiver slightly beneath his tight skin, beaded with sweat. The Lord informs Job that he is a warhorse, trained for combat, chosen for his great strength and intimidating presence. *'He charges into the fray. He laughs at fear, afraid of nothing; he does not shy away from the sword,'* (39:22). He recognises that here is an animal that scorns suffering, regarding it as occupational hazard. He cannot stand still when the trumpet sounds for he has to be in the thick of the battle; the greater the danger, the greater his excitement. Job draws back, picturing a troop of Sabean cavalrymen, attacking his workers and carrying off his oxen and donkeys. He imagines the terror of his camel herders, caught unawares by raiding parties of mounted Chaldeans who mercilessly cut them down. He's confused as he regards this powerful creature proudly standing before him. 'Why does God give such power and strength to those so easily manipulated?'

He recalled times when he'd been afraid, confronted by gangs of youths, thugs who just enjoyed getting into fights; easily led into a life of crime. Reckless, they paid no heed to the hurt they caused, yet God allowed them seemingly to flourish, their temerity striking fear into the hearts of those who would oppose them. Yet were they simply like the horse, a power that could be turned either way, to the good or the bad. Was not the real enemy the controlling influence that drove them to fight by playing on their cravings? He'd wanted God to punish those who had attacked his men, but now he pitied them also, for they had not the wisdom to know they were being swayed by sin. God would indeed judge them, but Job was beginning to understand why God might want to delay that time to bring them to their senses and repentance.

Job could not condone the recklessness of the horse or the carelessness of the ostrich, but he could see firstly that it was part of their inherent nature and secondly that despite their proclivity to sin God still saw good in them, blessing them with children and strength for their preservation.

The Eagle and the Hawk

Lost in thought, Job watches the seasons change with summer turning to fall and then to winter. He sees a lone hawk suddenly take flight and leave her nest migrating south for better hunting.

'Does the hawk take flight by your wisdom and spread his wings to the south?' (39:26) God whispers. As she fades from sight, Job wonders what dangers she will encounter on her arduous journey and indeed whether she will return.

Without a word, Job is led to God's final exhibit in the heart of the mountains. In the clear blue sky, he spies an eagle soaring on the updraft from a steep mountain ridge.

'Does the eagle soar at your command and build his nest on high?' God queries. Circling lazily in the sky, the eagle spots a rabbit,

far below, scurrying across a broad expanse of grass. In one smooth motion, the eagle swoops, grasps its prey in powerful talons and flies off to a nest high up on the side of a rocky outcrop. The Lord continues,

> *'he dwells on a cliff and stays there at night;*
> *a rocky crag is his stronghold.*
> *From there he detects his food;*
> *his eyes detect it from afar.'*   Job 39:28-29

Job watches without comment as the eagle feeds the chicks with his fresh kill. Both hawk and eagle show wisdom in obeying the commands of God and responding to changing circumstances with prudence. They do not hunt at night when their acute eyesight is impaired by darkness and the eagle builds his nest in crags, inaccessible to predator and prying eye. Both accept difficulty and hardship for the sake of a greater good; unlike the warhorse and ostrich, they avoid unnecessary danger and seek to nurture their young. However, 'nature is red in tooth and claw[1],' which sat uneasily with Job for the Lord had forbidden the eating of blood (Leviticus 17:10-12), as it was the blood that made atonement for one's life. Even in those creatures endowed with divine wisdom there was a natural tendency to sin.

The Wisdom of the Cross

Reflecting on these exhibits it appears that God endows all his creatures with various gifts and qualities. To some he gives speed, to others strength, to still others sensibility and so on without limit, for God's gifts are as diverse as is his creation. All these are given impartially for the common good and the supreme benefit of each creature regardless of any inborn inclinations. Applied to humanity, it can be inferred that whilst all are born outside of Eden and under judgement, God still endows us with unique gifts and abilities, which may use for our benefit and enjoyment. Even when we use these gifts inadvisably or to the detriment of others, still the Lord declines to withdraw his favour. There may be times when our children dismay us by their actions or misguided choices. In such cases a parent may impose sanctions until the child makes amends. Alternatively, a parent may seek to support, advise and suffer alongside their child, despite their misgiving, in the hope of strengthening their relationship and bringing their child to a place of greater blessing. In the same way, God, in his wisdom, takes our impropriety and disgrace upon himself, whilst continuing to sustain and empower us.

It is not possible to overstate the harm and suffering experienced by victims of abuse and violence, and one may justifiably question how a loving God could allow their aggressors to exert such power without restraint. The Lord gives no clear answer, but it is to be understood that God is Father of both victim and aggressor; his heart breaks at the hurt caused to the one and the wickedness displayed by the other. Within this impossible dilemma we see the wisdom of the cross, whereby God sends his only begotten Son, an innocent Lamb, to be our atoning sacrifice. Through Christ's death on the cross the victim finds justice and the aggressor can be justified as all the sins of the world are heaped upon our Saviour's shoulders. Again, through Christ's death on the cross, God's justice is satisfied and we are all justified through faith in Jesus (Romans 3:26). Through the wisdom of the cross all are reconciled to one another and to God!

The fear of the Lord

In the final analysis we must accept that we cannot fully understand God's wisdom in allowing suffering, but we can learn to walk in the fear of the Lord. God sees the good in even the worst of us and he recognises sin in even the best of us. All alike require his mercy in forgiveness and his grace that we might endure in adversity. Job has come to realise that even the wisest cannot live happily without complete dependence on God. The eagle and the hawk are endowed with great wisdom, yet even they cannot ensure their young will be kept safe and grow up to be good parents. They are as dependent on God for all their needs as are the horse and the ostrich. In just the same way, the wisdom of humanity, even at its height, is incidental to our need of God's mercy and grace. God gives his gift of wisdom to all as he chooses; to some he may give great understanding, whilst to others very little, but whether great or small, all must walk in the fear of the Lord – all must look to God for salvation! In all our suffering it is essential that we do not focus our pain on blaming others for their neglect or recklessness, or even their lack of foresight, but that we look to the cross, where we find God's answer to our suffering. There is a place for seeking justice in our courts when crimes are committed against us, but there is also a place for receiving justice and salvation at the foot of the cross – and here we find life and hope and peace. Let us not forgo the cross in our passion to get to the courts!

Seeing our potential

Many of us are who we are, because someone, sometime, believed in us, saw our potential and invested himself or herself in us, when no one else seemed to care or to have the time. Left to our own devices, where would we have been today? In the same way, God is gracious to us, investing in us, blessing us and loving us, even when we least deserve it. We see this perhaps most clearly in the release of Barabbas, by God's design, as Jesus is sent to the cross (Luke 23:18-25). If this is the case, should we be jealous of others whom the Lord chooses to bless? How do you feel when the 'ostriches' of this world, those who are careless with their lives as well as the lives of others, receive favour from the Lord? Do you resent their good fortune or do you rejoice with them in having such a merciful God? How do we feel when the 'horses' of this world, those who show little regard for the weak, are successful and triumphant, whilst those who, like the hawk, caring for and considerate of those under their care struggle for survival? Do we rail against the Lord and doubt his goodness?

As we face head on the perplexities of our world, our God speaks to Job and to us of his compassion and his wisdom. He asks us all, 'will you trust me?' Will you trust me to care for you and provide for you cherish, as I care and provide for all my creation? Will you trust me to take up your cause, to free you to be who I created you to be? Will you trust me to discipline and guide you? Will you accept the responsibilities I give you? Will you trust me with all the unfairness of life, when you see the careless prosper, the carefree victorious and the caring or careworn hungry? Will you put your faith in me because you are my child and I am your Father?

1.   Tennyson, A. (1849) 'In Memoriam A.H.H', Canto 56

CHAPTER 16

Can you save? (Job 40:1-42:6)

God has revealed to Job his immeasurable power, his
unfathomable wisdom and his all consuming love and
compassion for all of his creation. Job has seen that far from
being distant and indifferent, God is intimately involved in
and fully committed to all that he has made. This is true
especially of humanity, through whom all creation will one day
be liberated from its bondage to death and decay. Furthermore,
Job has come to understand that suffering is an indispensible
part of life within a fallen world, and does not mean that God
is powerless, without compassion or unjust. Indeed, the Lord
enters into our struggles, bearing our burdens and crying our
tears. As a master craftsman he takes our broken dreams and
builds them into his glorious vision for our lives; as a surgeon
he cleans our wounds and heals our bodies that we may live
again; as a compassionate Father he takes all our despair and

turns it into hope, dispelling our fear and showering us with his loving grace.

Can you control your life?

We began Job's story with Satan's accusation that Job only served God for what he got out of it, the blessings and the protection. Satan argued that Job didn't worship God purely for who he is. It was this assertion that precipitated all Job's suffering. In taking Job on a tour of his creation God has revealed his glory and Job has fallen in worship before him declaring, *'I am unworthy – how can I reply to you? I put my hand over my mouth. I spoke once, but I have no answer – twice, but I will say no more'* (40:4,5). No longer will he complain at the way God dispenses justice, no longer will he question God's impartiality towards the wicked. Like the psalmist Job's understanding has been transformed by being in the presence of the Lord,

> *'When my heart was grieved and my spirit embittered*
> *I was senseless and ignorant like a brute beast*
> *before you.*
> *Yet I am always with you; you hold me by my right*
> *hand.*
> *You guide me with your counsel*
> *and afterwards you will take me into glory.*
> *Who have I in heaven but you?*
> *And earth has nothing I desire besides you.*
> *My flesh and my heart may fail,*
> *but God is the strength of my heart*
> *and my portion forever'* Psalm 73:21-26

Job realises how blind he has been to God's loving purposes in his life. He has begun to understand that at the deepest level, in his heart of hearts, he hasn't fully trusted God with his life, particularly with regard to his suffering. More specifically, he still hasn't arrived at that point where he feels he can repudiate his own belief in his own righteousness as a means to earning his own salvation. This is now the real issue for Job, for although he would be the first to acknowledge that he is not perfect, for no mortal is, nevertheless he has put heavy store against his godly life, his integrity, purity and compassion (Job 31),

> *'if I have walked in falsehood*
> *Or my foot has hurried after deceit –*
> *Let God weigh me in honest scales*
> *And he will know that I am blameless'*
>
> Job 31:5,6

His response to God has always been, 'tell me what to do and I'll do it! Say jump and I'll say, how high?' In regard to his life, there is nothing more he could have done; he has kept all the law as far as is humanly possible. Consequently, God must be wholly unjust to have allowed this attack on his person. It is this belief in himself that God now takes up with Job,

> *'Would you discredit my justice?*
> *Would you condemn me to justify yourself?*
> *Do you have an arm like God's and can your voice*
> *thunder like his?*
> *… then unleash the fury of your wrath…*
> *and I will admit to you that your own right hand*
> *can save you'*   (Job 40: 7-14).

The Lord remonstrates with him not just to show him whose boss, but also to open Job's eyes to his predicament and need. 'Oh yes, Job,' says the Lord, 'you can complain and hurl your abuse at me, but have you in fact any power at all over your life?' All his life Job has been blessed with material wealth and status that has caused him to believe he can control his own life and command the obedience of others. However, the truth is, he has no power to determine his own destiny and he certainly cannot bring judgment on the proud and wicked (40:12). The Lord has previously called upon Job to acknowledge his glory and to trust in him. Now, he is asking Job to look upon himself, his weakness and powerlessness, and in the light of this, to decide if he is able to save himself.

The Behemoth

God begins to reveal this truth by bringing Job to the main lobby of his museum of creation, where stands in breathtaking majesty a creature of awesome size and power - the Behemoth. This is no modern day creature; its description is more akin to a Brontosaurus, though some reference is made to a hippopotamus. This magnificent beast towers above Job and he has to duck quickly as its cedar-like tail, sweeps powerfully over his head. The Behemoth's legs are like the trunks of oak trees, hardened with muscle and sinew, and covered with a tough ridged skin. Without haste the Behemoth turns to walk away, his feet pounding the earth, sending shockwaves through the ground. The Behemoth is presented to Job as the alpha male of creation, without equal, first among the works of God. Like the Brontosaurus, he may feed on grass but

'what strength he has in his loins,
what power in the muscles of his belly!
His tail sways like a cedar, the sinews of his thighs
are close knit.
His bones are tubes of bronze, his limbs like rods
of iron'   Job 40:16-18

God informs Job, that the hills bring the Behemoth their produce and all the wild animals feel so secure around him that they play nearby (40:20). He is not seen by anyone as he lies under the lotus leaves, yet his presence is always felt. In modern idiom, the Behemoth is portrayed as a noble king to whom tribute is to be paid and who provides security and peace throughout his land, that all may prosper and flourish under his bountiful shadow. So powerful is the Behemoth that even when the waters rage against his mouth, he is not alarmed – he is secure and untroubled. He is the undisputed king and he reigns supreme over all his creation (40:24).

As Job contemplates this noble creature, he senses the Lord asking him: Are you as mighty as the Behemoth? Are you king over all you survey? Do others put their security in you? Are you confident when the waters rise over your head? Do you really think you have the power to save yourself, and that you don't need the Lord? Are you like King Nebuchadnezzar, who in his pride claimed that he had built up Babylon through his own power and glory? Before those words left his lips he was brought low by the Lord and driven from people to eat grass like cattle (Daniel 4:28-35). Yet, after the Lord restored him to his former glory, Nebuchadnezzar raised his eyes towards heaven and praised the Most High saying,

'His dominion is an eternal dominion;
his kingdom endures from generation to generation.
All the peoples of the earth are regarded as nothing.
He does as he pleases with the powers of heaven
and the peoples of the earth.
No one can hold back his hand or say to him,
'What have you done?...
and those who walk in pride he is able to humble'

Daniel 4:34-35,37

Where is the superman?

Job gazes upon the Behemoth and, like Nebuchadnezzar, is humbled before the glory and dominion of God. I picture Job looking down at the reality of his situation, the ashes around him – the sum total of his power without the Lord. Job is not like the Behemoth for without God he can do nothing; he is nothing! In our suffering we obtain a true glimpse of who we are without the power and grace of God enfolding us and sustaining us. I remember a story of a young boy who would run around the house in his superman costume claiming his invincibility. He could do anything for he had incredible strength and speed – he could even fly! Then one day, his mother found him huddled in a corner of his bedroom crying. It was time for him to go to nursery and he was frightened – he didn't want to go, because there were children at his nursery who bullied him. His mother said, 'where's my brave superman?' The little boy replied, 'I'm only superman when I have my costume on.' Likewise, when we don our suits to go to work, or put on our make-up in the morning, we feel ready to face the world. But at the end of the day, when it's all stripped away, what we are left with is our vulnerability – and our fears.

When we feel well, when we are successful at what we do, when our family is thriving and our children excelling, we are on top of the world – and it's easy to think it's our doing! But when it's stripped away, when a competitor exposes our weakness, when we get hurt, when God removes his 'superman garment' from us what are we left with?

Through the illustration of the Behemoth the Almighty has shown Job that without God, he is powerless to save himself. The Lord also provides Job and ourselves with a description of the kingdom of heaven, where God rules with justice and his people dwell in peace and security, having nothing to fear, as the prophet Isaiah declares

> *'The wolf will live with the lamb,*
> *The leopard will lie down with the goat,*
> *The calf and the lion and the yearling together;*
> *And a little child will lead them.*
> *The cow will feed with the bear,*
> *Their young will lie down together,*
> *And the lion will eat straw like the ox…*
> *They will neither harm nor destroy*
> *On all my holy mountain,*
> *For the earth will be full of the knowledge of the Lord*
> *As the waters cover the sea'*   Isaiah 11:6-9

Job, like us all, is living in the East, alienated from God's presence, in a world enslaved to fear by sin and death. In showing him the Behemoth, God is revealing to Job the utopia that he desires, a place where there is no more suffering or pain or death. He feels God is asking him, 'Can you create such a kingdom? If not will you trust me? Will you come to me that I may give it freely to you?

Leviathan

Before Job can draw breath, the Lord whisks him away to a final room buried deep in the bowels of the museum. They approach the entrance and Job instinctively draws back as a deafening roar fills the air. The Lord pushes Job inside and he is confronted by leviathan, a beast terrifying in appearance; the most fearsome predator ever to stalk the earth. Whereas the Behemoth created an atmosphere of tranquillity and security, leviathan instils only fear and trepidation. As Job gazes upon this monster the Lord asks him whether he feels he can capture him and force him to his knees,

> *'Can you put a cord through his nose*
> *or pierce his jaw with a hook?*
> *Will he keep begging you for mercy?*
> *Will he speak to you with gentle words?*
> *Will he make an agreement with you*
> *for you to take him as your slave for life?'*

Job 41:2-4

God is asking Job if he can control leviathan, house train him, domesticate him like his donkeys, or as he has tried to do with the Almighty? The Lord recognises that Job, like us, wants a God whom he can understand, tame, even control, but that's not going to happen. God is God and he is answerable to no-one. So says the Lord, *'No-one is fierce enough to rouse [leviathan], who then is able to stand against me? Who has a claim against me that I must pay? Everything under heaven belongs to me'* (41:10,11). If Job can take on leviathan and win, then maybe, just maybe he might have a slim chance of standing in defiance of God, but if not why should Job continue to put hope in his own power to save.

If Job should need more proof as to his inability to save himself, a more complete revelation of leviathan is given, as he is reluctantly ushered closer. Job's heart begins to pound uncontrollably with fear for this monster before him is unstoppable. The mere sight of him, like his breath, is overpowering. His mouth is ringed with fearsome teeth and the toughened scales on his back are like row upon row of armoured shields tightly sealed together. He snorts, throwing out flashes of light; smoke pours from his nostrils, firebrands stream from his mouth. His chest is hard as rock; sword, spear nor arrow can penetrate or even scratch the surface. He treats iron and bronze as if they were straw and hay. Nothing on earth is his equal – he is a creature without fear and the destroyer of life. He is king over all that are proud. As Job contemplates leviathan, the Lord whispers, 'can you really stand up to him? Can you look death in the face and not be afraid?

Who will you choose?

If the imagery of the Behemoth is God's kingdom then leviathan is death, confrontation with Satan. In this last tour of God's museum of creation, the Lord is laying before Job a choice between dwelling under the shadow of the Behemoth or standing against leviathan. As Moses spoke to the people of Israel saying, *'see, I set before you today life and prosperity, death and destruction'* (Deuteronomy 30:15), so God has set before Job the Behemoth, promising a kingdom of life and peace, and leviathan who is the harbinger of death. If Job wants to deny God's sovereignty and go his own way, he must be prepared to take on death itself. Alternatively if he desires to live under the gracious rule of God, he must relinquish his firmly held belief that his integrity and righteousness alone, or even in part, can save him. He must throw himself completely and utterly upon the mercy and grace of God.

So often, like Job, even though we may fervently proclaim that we have no other God and that we trust in Jesus alone for salvation, a close examination will reveal that in fact we also rely on ourselves, on our integrity, our godliness and our determination to earn a place in heaven. If salvation is climbing over a fence that is too high for us, then Jesus is the one who gives us a leg up. If salvation is crossing a chasm that is too wide, then Jesus extends his arm a few inches, enough for us to grab hold and pull ourselves across. But the truth is that God's holiness is as high above ours as the moon is above the earth, and we can never attain to it. Even if the most godly man who ever lived, in this example, was the height of Everest above all others, still that would count as little advantage in attaining the standard of holiness required: In his own strength and through his own righteousness he would be as close to attaining salvation as he is to touching the moon!

Job is a righteous man, devout and godly in every way and he should be allowed to take some credit for his conduct. So it is that Almighty God speaks his name with pride in the courts of heaven as his servant. However, as regards salvation, before God he is no different to anyone else, for all our deeds are as filthy rags – his and our only hope is to place all our trust in God and the salvation he alone offers, as the Lord himself declares,

'Turn to me and be saved, all you ends of the earth;
for I am God, and there is no other.
By myself I have sworn, my mouth has uttered in
all integrity a word that will not be revoked:
before me every knee will bow; by me every tongue
will swear.
They will say of me,
'In the Lord alone are righteousness and strength'

Isaiah 45:22-24

Where do you place your confidence?

It is not just our own suffering that Job represents. His suffering is that of individuals, of communities, of nations and indeed of the whole world. We live in a state of brokenness and alienation and the perennial question is 'what are we to do?' The truth is there is no one who can save us but God alone. We can deceive ourselves into thinking we have power or ingenuity to solve all our problems. Yet only God can hold captive leviathan, only God can create the Behemoth. If we turn from God, then we turn from all hope of salvation. God has presented Job and ourselves with a choice; we all stand at a crossroads. After all you have seen of God's majesty, love and compassion will you choose to trust him and follow him? He has *'placed before you an open door that no-one can shut'* (Revelation 3:7), that you might enter into the joy of his kingdom forever. No one can deny you entry and no one can lay down special terms and conditions for acceptance. All you need do is lay aside your faith in your own good works and your confidence in your religious background, and take hold of the righteousness that is offered you in Christ.

In his parable of the wedding banquet our Lord spoke of the man who tried to enter without wearing the wedding clothes provided (Matthew 22:1-13), indicating that although all are freely invited, only those who clothe themselves with Christ's righteousness will be admitted. Similarly, the apostle Paul renounced his Israelite pedigree and all his religious works declaring, *'I consider them rubbish, that I may gain Christ and be found in him, not having a righteousness of my own that comes from the law, but that which is through faith in Christ – the righteousness that comes from God and is by faith'* (Philippians 3:8,9).

Can you truly say with the apostle that you place no confidence in your Christian heritage, your church attendance or your religious zeal? These may be good indications of your commitment to God and your love for the Lord but they can never be put forward to merit your justification. It is by faith in Christ alone that we are counted as righteous before almighty God. So Paul proclaims, *'if you confess with your mouth, 'Jesus is Lord,' and believe in your heart that God raised him from the dead, you will be saved,'* (Romans 10:9). For it is our acknowledgement of his Lordship over our lives and our assurance of his satisfaction for our sin that we receive the gift of eternal life and our inheritance in heaven.

In response to these revelations from God, Job cries out,

> *'My ears had heard of you but now my eyes have seen you.*
> *Therefore I despise myself and repent in dust and ashes'*
> Job 42:5,6

Job has fully surrendered all that he is, all his future and all his past, to God! His despair is forgotten, his hope is renewed, his salvation is guaranteed. If you are going through difficult times, look to the glory of the Lord, who has called you to be his child. Do not be like Peter and focus on the waves, but look to Jesus, gaze into his face, behold his glory and know that he will deliver you in due time and bring you safely to shore. God is asking you today, the very deepest of questions, 'Do you trust me?' The very same question Jesus put to his disciples when they were being tossed about by the storm, *'Why are you so afraid? Do you still have no faith?'* (Mark 4:40). How will you answer him?

CHAPTER 17

Salvation (Job 42:7-17)

Having witnessed Job's despair, wrestled alongside his fight for faith and walked with Job through God's museum, what conclusions have we reached concerning the reasons for our suffering? We have seen that Job is not being punished for wrongdoing; neither is God using him as a pawn in some cruel contest with Satan. God loves Job and he does not delight in Job's affliction nor does he desire to hurt Job needlessly. All God's designs are for Job's benefit, to exalt Job before the courts of heaven, to deepen and enrich his fellowship with God, to enhance his faith in God's love and provision and to effect his full salvation. Job's suffering is a witness to the world of the reality of judgement, the inadequacy of moral goodness as a means of salvation and a call to repentance and faith. Through Job's affliction God reveals the anticipated passion of his own Son, our saviour Jesus Christ, through whom all people can be reconciled to God through faith in his death and resurrection.

Suffering is our God given opportunity

Applying this to ourselves, and looking back to the sacrifice of Christ, we can say that God permits us to suffer that he might perfect us in Christ and Christ in us, that we might wholeheartedly entrust our lives to him in faith in all our situations, that we might become mature in Christ, sanctified by the Spirit and that our lives might be a witness to the glory of God and a call to all people to repent and believe in the salvation of God.

Suffering is our God given opportunity to go deeper in our relationship with God for the Lord is not content until he fully has your heart, so that he can bless you with all his goodness and love. Suffering is our God given opportunity to learn how to live by grace and not by works, to rest in his love rather than wrestle in fear. Suffering is our God given opportunity to witness to our faith and through our perseverance in affliction to draw others to Jesus. Suffering is our God given opportunity to share in the sufferings of Christ that we may participate in the glory of his resurrection. Suffering is our God given opportunity to inherit our salvation in Christ. In saying this I'm all too aware of how weak these explanations can seem when confronted by your pain, how frightening it can be to hand over your whole to God and how inadequate you may feel as a witness for Christ. It is for this reason, after all the explanations have been presented, that God simply reveals himself to Job and asks the question, 'Do you trust me?' It is that question and only that question we need to answer for ourselves. To help us further, in this final chapter, we are given a glimpse of our future glory in Christ, through the exaltation of Job.

Job is restored

In the New International Version the last verses of Job are rather unhelpfully sub-titled 'epilogue', as though the section simply marks the end of Job's story. However, to see these verses in this way is to reduce the theology of Job's suffering to a 'Cinderella' style fantasy that for many holds little credibility in the real world. Following times of trial it is rare we are even partially restored to our former situation, so Job's restoration seems trite and unrealistic. At face value it even seems to erode the authenticity of the whole account. However, as we have seen, we need to keep in view the prophetic and anticipatory witness to Christ through Job's experience, remembering that all scripture is written for our instruction and encouragement (Romans 15:4). Throughout Job's suffering, God has spoken of redemption and forgiveness, so it should not surprise us that in these closing verses God reveals to us aspects of our salvation in Christ. In considering Job's restoration, it is helpful to continue the imagery of the Horniman museum, with a final room entitled 'Salvation,' into which the Lord now leads us. The room is of simple rectangular design and arranged in the style of an art gallery with three wall-sized oil paintings each depicting a scene from Job's restoration.

Job is Justified

Our first painting hangs on the wall facing east and is simply titled, 'Job is justified.' The scene portrays a man sat upon a heap of ashes, dressed in rags and covered from head to toe with painful sores. Behind him can be seen several gravestones inscribed with the names of his children and, in the far distance, bands of raiders herding away his herds and flocks. To the untutored eye, it is a sight of abject misery, and yet curiously despite his desolate appearance, he is smiling and his face radiates hope and love for God. A golden beam of light is seen bursting through the clouds, bathing Job in a holy radiance while a powerful voice, like the sound of many waters, can be heard commending him as a servant of God. To the left hand side of Job stands a black hooded figure, his accuser, whose mouth has been sealed shut. All around are gathered local townsfolk, men, women and children who have come to witness a quite extraordinary event; above are hosts of angels and seraphim gazing down inquisitively. Making their way slowly through the crowd, Eliphaz, Bildad and Zophar can be seen driving before them seven bulls and seven rams to be offered in sacrifice as a burnt offering to the Lord. The look on their faces is a story in itself – they have been chastened and severely rebuked by the Lord for speaking falsely and accusing their friend of wickedness. Humiliated and fearful, they each in turn present their sacrifices to Job and requesting his prayers on their behalf.

Listening to the audio recording on your headset, the voice explains that through his confession Job is exalted before his friends, neighbours and all the hosts of heaven. At the beginning of Job's story, God spoke with Satan, the accuser, declaring Job to be his servant, saying on two occasions, *'there is no one on earth like him. He is blameless and upright, a man who fears God and shuns evil'* (Job 1:8, 2:3). At that time, Job was completely unaware of that conversation and had no knowledge of his high standing in God's eyes. Now, following his good confession (42:5,6) the Lord publicly reaffirms before all creation, four times in quick succession, that Job is his true servant; *'You have not spoken... as my servant Job has,'* (42:7) *'go to my servant Job,'* (42:8) *'my servant Job will pray for you,'* (42:8) *'you have not spoken of me... as my servant Job has'* (42:8). Four times, symbolising completeness and entirety, Almighty God declares *'My servant Job.'* 'He's the man! Everyone look to him!' – and Satan is silent! There is no objection he can raise, no case he can bring against him. As the apostle Paul declares, *'Who will bring any charge against those whom God has chosen? It is God who justifies'* (Romans 8:33).

Your eyes stray to this man who has endured such suffering, now being extolled by God. Perhaps you are reminded of the angel's revelation to Zechariah concerning the high priest Joshua standing in filthy rags before the Lord, with Satan on his right ready to accuse him (Zechariah 3). Joshua's rags are taken away, symbolizing the removal of sin, and clean clothes placed upon him, as God declares him righteous in his sight. You recall the Lord's rebuke of Satan, *'is not this man a burning stick snatched from the fire,'* (Zechariah 3:2). Job has been left in the hands of Satan, for him to do his worst, but never once has Job denied his Lord, never once has he cursed God. Now the Lord almighty has plucked him from the ashes and pronounced him justified before the courts of heaven!

In Job we have the fledgling gospel of Jesus

The audio recording continues to explain that whilst praising his servant Job, God simultaneously rebukes Eliphaz and his two friends for accusing Job of wickedness when they should have accepted his testimony to his innocence. In so doing they had spoken falsely of God, presenting him as a tyrant, rather than a gracious Father who longs to redeem his children and restore them to his glorious presence. Furthermore, they should have realized that Job's suffering was also a call for them to seek after the Lord, since he was more righteous than they (Proverbs 11:31) and they were necessarily under the same judgement. In accusing Job they had elevated themselves and become blind to their own sin. As a result, they are commanded to offer a burnt offering and Job will act as priest, interceding on their behalf (42:8). As Job cried out for a mediator between himself and God, so now he becomes the mediator for his friends. From his place among the ashes Job has been raised up like a phoenix. Justified and exalted to the priesthood with authority to intercede on behalf of his friends.

In Job's story we are to see God's plan of salvation, for just as Job's suffering can be viewed as a foreshadowing of the passion of Christ, so Job's vindication and exaltation may be regarded as anticipating the resurrection and ascension of our Lord (Ephesians 2:19-21). More explicitly, through the account of Job, we understand that God's righteous servant, who is to come, will be handed over to Satan and subjected to suffering. Through his obedience and faith he will silence his accuser, and God will exalt and glorify him (Philippians 2:1-11). In his exaltation he will be made a priest and called upon to intercede on behalf of his friends – in Job we have the fledging gospel of Jesus Christ!

As we reflect on the scene before us and see in Job, a foreshadowing of Christ, we witness our own justification when the Lord comes in judgement. On that day he will call us to stand before him, perhaps broken and destitute, and surrounded by all the hosts of heaven, our Lord will say, *'Well done good and faithful servant'* (Matthew 5:21). 'But Lord,' you will say, 'I have struggled, I am in rags, I have spent my years in tears.' And he will reply, 'My son, my daughter, you have kept the faith, you have finished the race, I have displayed my rainbow of grace through your tears, come and share your Father's happiness.' In that moment all our distress will be forgotten as he wipes away our tears and gently takes us in his arms. The years will fall from us as he removes our rags and replaces them with glorious robes of white. Then he write with his finger on our foreheads, 'holy to the Lord,' and place upon our heads a crown of gold, before leading us by the hand into the holy city of God.

We live in the time between our salvation and the Lord's return

It has been observed that Job was not restored until after he prayed for his friends. This doesn't mean that he needed to 'earn' his salvation by obeying God's command. Rather it was intended by the Lord to teach us all that we should not use our circumstances as a measure of our acceptance before God. The essential point is that Job's response towards his suffering changed dramatically through his being with the Lord, even though his situation remained unchanged. No longer did he feel sorry for himself, ruing the day of his birth and demanding justice. Instead, he was ready to pray for his friends despite still being covered in sores and without any material prospects. Job did not need to know the reasons for his suffering, or indeed why he was suffering still, for he had come to a point where he trusted the Lord and was content to rest under his sovereign rule. He had come to understand with the apostle Paul that God's grace is sufficient for him and that God's power is made perfect in weakness (2 Corinthians 12:9).

So it is with us in the trials and hardships we face. The Lord may not immediately deliver us, nor answer all our questions, but he will be gracious to us and call us to pray and minister to those around us. As we pass through times of trial it is essential that we realise we live in the time between our salvation and the Lord's return. Although, as believers in Jesus, we have been declared righteous through our faith, we still live in the East; we will not be fully set free from the power of sin and death until the day the Lord comes in glory to give us new resurrection bodies (1 Corinthians 15:50-58). In the meantime, we are called by God to trust in him, to serve him joyfully and to pray for our friends that they may come to faith and a deeper understanding of God's grace at work in their lives.

Being a servant of God

As we return to Job still sitting among the ashes and his friends having to seek his prayers on their behalf, his neighbours realise Job was innocent all the time and God accepted him despite his suffering! Job is both righteous and a priest of the Lord. There are occasions when we can be fooled into thinking that because people are suffering they are somehow less acceptable to God and certainly unable to do anything for us. How wrong we are if we ever think that! I remember attending the bedside of a woman with terminal cancer who had but days to live.

As her parish priest I went to minister to her, but I came away with the knowledge that she had ministered to me. Despite her obvious suffering, I knew I was in the presence of God and her prayers were coming from a heart fully submitted to Christ and was consumed with love for him (Hebrews 5:7). I left her more blessed than I had arrived!

Such experiences can help us understand more fully the character of the one God calls saying, *'you are my servant... in whom I will display my splendour'* (Isaiah 49:3). It is not a position we can apply for on an equal opportunities basis, sending our CV to God with a list of our qualifications, talents and abilities. Furthermore, we do not cease to be servants when we are no longer able to serve God in the way we used to do. Many Christians feel that as they grow older and more frail they become less useful to God and maybe even a hindrance to his purposes. Consequently, they begin to take a back seat in church, saying its now time for the younger members to take more responsibility. But being a servant is not so much about what we do as where we dwell, for the true servant of God is always in Christ. As our Lord said to his disciples in the Upper room, *'Remain in me and I will remain in you. No branch can bear fruit by itself; it must remain in the vine. Neither can you bear fruit unless you remain in me'* (John 15:4). The requirement for being a servant is to remain in Christ, for just as he is our righteousness, so is he our service. As Mary was commended for her actions over Martha who was running around trying to serve (Luke 10:38-42), so we must learn that waiting upon the Lord, remaining in him is always our first calling – and that is something for which we are never too old!

Job is comforted

The Lord now directs us to the second oil painting positioned on the west wall entitled 'Job is comforted'. The scene focuses once more upon Job as the central figure, this time standing tall at the head of a large table, laid in preparation for a great banquet. All trace of his affliction has gone and he radiates health and vitality. Around the table all of Job's brothers, sisters and other family members, are gathering, offering words of comfort and consolation. As they approach many look apologetic, even guilty, conscious of the ill feelings they had harboured previously towards this godly man. They had abandoned him in his hour of need, but Job shows no sign of bearing a grudge, generously welcoming them with outstretched arms and hugging them to his chest. He bends to whisper in their ear, 'shalom,' entreating them to sit and eat with him. As each takes a seat around the great table, they lean forward to present Job with a piece of silver and a gold ring.

Once again, the audio recording provides some explanation of the scene: 'Conscious they had abandoned him, believing him to be punished by God, his family and friends return offering comfort and consolation. They each present him with gifts of silver and gold, signifying his acceptance once more into the family and a bestowal of blessing.' It is a beautiful picture of reconciliation and restoration. The painting evokes echoes of the Lord Jesus, who following his resurrection called his disciples to himself and spoke to them his words of peace. Those who had previously deserted and abandoned him in his hour of need, those who had stood back while he was humiliated and crucified were welcomed to eat with him (Luke 24:36-49). It also surely foreshadows the Last Supper in which our Lord, anticipating his suffering and resurrection, institutes a new covenant between God and humanity declaring, *'this is my blood of the covenant, which is poured out for many for the forgiveness of sins'* (Matthew 26:28). Again, it looks ahead to the feast that awaits us in heaven and a reminder of our Lord's words at the Passover to his disciples, *'I tell you, I will not drink of this fruit of the vine from now on until that day when I drink it anew with you in my Father's kingdom,'* (Matthew 26:29).

Combining this imagery, we are to see in this painting a distant prophesy of our reconciliation, whereby we come humbly before the exalted Christ, and confessing our sin receive his gracious invitation to sit and eat with him. As he welcomes us into his presence so we will cast our crowns before him in reverent praise and adoration. As he takes us in his arms, he will wipe away our every tear and whisper in our ear, 'shalom – come and share my Father's happiness.' Then we will be with our Lord forever, in the glory of heaven, Eden restored – no more to be people of the East.

Job's children

Our final portrait hangs on the North wall directly before us, and is a picture of abundance and prosperity. In the background flocks of sheep and large herds of cattle can be seen grazing peacefully on lush pastures. Further afield caravans of camels make their way across the desert carrying Job's wealth to distant lands, whilst nearer by, many hundreds of donkeys are seen bearing Job's wares to the local towns and markets. In the foreground we see Job himself, surrounded by his sons and daughters, and their sons and daughters, and their sons and daughters – all four generations, testifying to the faithfulness of God. However, this time it is not Job but his daughters who are centre stage, arrayed in flowing white wedding gowns with golden crowns upon their heads. Below the portrait is a gold plaque inscribed with their names, 'Jemimah, Keziah and Keren-Happuch.'

In your ear, you hear someone reading familiar verses from the prophesy of Isaiah,

> *'Lift up your eyes and look about you:*
> *All assemble and come to you;*
> *Your sons come from afar,*
> *And your daughters are carried on the arm.*
> *Then you will look and be radiant,*
> *Your heart will throb and swell with joy;*
> *The wealth of the seas will be brought to you,*
> *To you the riches of the nations will come.*
> *Herds of camels will cover your land...*
> *And all Sheba will come bearing gold and incense*
> *And proclaiming the praise of the Lord.*
> *All Kedar's flocks will be gathered to you...*
> *And I will adorn my glorious temple'*
>
> Isaiah 60:4-7

Job is given fourteen thousand sheep, six thousand camels, a thousand yoke of oxen and a thousand donkeys: twice all he had before his trial, with echoes of Isaiah 40:1,2. If he was blessed before, he is now doubly blessed, indicative of him receiving the inheritance of heaven. He has seven sons and three daughters, once again depicting perfection and completeness, but it is his daughters who alone are named as, Jemimah, meaning pure, Keziah, identified as Cassia or Cinnamon, and Keren-Happuch, which is translated 'dark eyes.' These names are highly significant, especially when considered as one: Jemimah, or pure, speaks for itself; Cassia and Cinnamon were highly prized fragrances, whilst Keren-Happuch, literally translated 'horn of paint,' referred to the dark eye shadow women used to paint around their eyes to heighten their attractiveness. Together they are altogether lovely, and we are informed they are the most beautiful women in the land (42:15). On one level they symbolise Job's life being perfected through his suffering, and being brought forth as gold (1 Peter 1:3-9). They reaffirm what we have already discovered that God takes our beginnings and makes us altogether glorious; he takes our despair and turns it into glorious hope; he takes our emptiness and fills it with his glorious abundance; he takes our grief and sadness and turns it into glorious joy. Job no longer fears for the future, he no longer worries about whether or not his children have inadvertently sinned. He spends his days rejoicing in the knowledge of God and delighting in the Lord's undeserved acts of mercy and grace towards him. He grows old seeing his children come to faith in the Lord to the fourth generation and his heart swells with joy in the Lord.

The Bride of Christ

On a deeper level we are to see that Job's daughters represent the Church, purified through trial and tribulation. Together they depict a glorious bride on her wedding day, entering into the palace of the king (Psalm 45, Song of Songs 4:11-15), altogether lovely, adorned with glory and majesty. In Job's daughters we are given a window into heaven and our own redemption as the bride of Christ, purified, justified and glorified.

'Then I saw a new heaven and a new earth,
for the first heaven and the first earth had passed
away.
I saw the Holy City, the new Jerusalem,
coming down out of heaven from God,
prepared as a bride beautifully dressed for her
husband.
And I heard a loud voice from the throne saying,
'Now the dwelling of God is with men, and he will
live with them.
He will wipe every tear from their eyes.
There will be no more mourning or crying or pain,
for the old order of things has passed away'

Revelation 21:1-6

The day of our redemption is drawing near, when we will be welcomed into the courts of heaven. At the moment perhaps all you can see is your suffering and pain, but on that day, you will receive the reward for your faith and perseverance. Look to Job and see the commendation he receives from the Lord. You too, if you stand firm, will be called forth in royal splendour. You will have your rags removed and be clothed in glorious robes of righteousness. You will bow before your God and he will lift up your head and anoint you with his blessing, saying 'Well done, good and faithful servant.' The courts of heaven will ring with praise and rejoicing at the sound of your name. Look to Job and see the comfort, the reconciliation and the peace he receives, for you too will be comforted, when you are greeted by those who have gone before you; those you have longed to see for so long – never to be parted again. You too will rejoice on seeing those you have prayed for and wept over come and shake your hand and thank you for your ministry in their lives, despite your trials. You too will hear the words of peace spoken by our Lord as he calls you to his banqueting table that you may feast with him. Look to Job and see the blessings of heaven that await you, the restoration of Eden, your marriage to the Lord Jesus, your glorious inheritance in Christ. Your eyes will behold God's new creation, glorious and eternal, and you will dwell in that beautiful place with the Lord forever. As Paul says, *'I pray that the eyes of your heart may be enlightened in order that you may know the hope to which he has called you, the riches of his glorious inheritance in the saints and his incomparably great power for us who believe'* (Ephesians 1:18,19). When you see around you all those you have prayed so earnestly for you over the years; when you look up and see the Holy City, coming down out of heaven like a bride beautifully dressed for her husband; when you hear a loud voice from the throne calling you forward, then you will know you are home. At that time you will forget your sufferings, for he will take you in his arms and wipe away your tears – and you will cast your crown before the Lord, your king, your glory and your salvation. Dear friend, the glory of heaven awaits you and you are the bride of Christ, altogether lovely.

Lightning Source UK Ltd.
Milton Keynes UK
UKOW07f2301261114

242238UK00001B/3/P